D1476328

TYPO HOLIC

FONT TO FORM

The function of graphical additions to words is more than about making a difference. Any atypical features would signify notions that are worth attending to. From customised outlines to their enriched forms, this section introduces letter art that comes in their unique and rational manners, ranging from drawings to print, construction to destruction, digital renderings to the abstraction of reality.

FOREWORD BY DAN TOBIN SMITH

It was when I first got asked to do a cover for *Creative Review* magazine back in 2005/6 that I got interested in typography in photography. I created a letter A for their *Annual* that year and as a result I started experimenting more with using perspective to create very accurate typography.

For my alphabet project I decided early on to use Helvetica as it was a simple typeface and it meant each letter, although being very different in approach would have the consistency of design amongst them.

I think it's the level of design perfection in the typography that makes them very satisfying objects to build in life and photograph. These typefaces have been refined and refined and the act of building them from scratch in reality adds a new dimension. I suppose in a way they become like sculptures once they are built and take on a new and distinct aesthetic. When you build to a very specific perspective you also have the accident of what has been created from different viewpoints. These viewpoints are inherently abstract and what you end up with is these slightly accidental and surreal landscapes, I love this element of the project.

I have always been drawn to the alphabet in illustration or photography. One of my favourites is Antonio Basoli's *Alfabeto Pittorico* (Pictorial Alphabet), a collection of fantasy architectural views, each containing an alphabet surrounded by objects bearing names with the same initial letter, created in

1839. Abelardo Morell had also made a lovely mini alphabetical image, *Water Alphabet*, in 1998 using just tiny pools of water on a table.

In most cases I use anamorphosis, or a distorted projection, to help me build types to a high level of accuracy. This was used in commercial photography, in subtler forms going back over the past 50 years as a way of refining composition in still life photography. People have been using linear perspective in art dating back to the early 15th century and you can see an early example of the use of actual anamorphosis in Hans Holbein's *The Ambassadors* in 1533. In photography, the earliest image I have found using anamorphosis dates back all the way to 1913, fairly early in photography's history, but it is also the most impressive in its scale of any photograph using anamorphosis. *The Human U.S. Shield* by Arthur S. Mole and John D. Thomasand consists of 30,000 officers and men of Camp Custer in Michigan making up an enormous U.S. shield on the grounds of the army camp. It is staggering in its scale and ambition and teams with the wonder found in the emerging medium of photography.

As a result of the first letter I shot in 2005, I have created probably hundreds of images using perspective and will continue to do so. I am half way through my alphabet project and each letter is different to the one before. Recently I have made one which is primarily a moving image and am in production with a further two which are primarily three dimensional pieces in their own right.

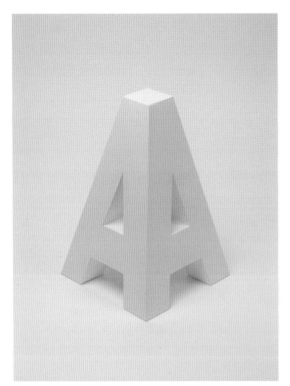

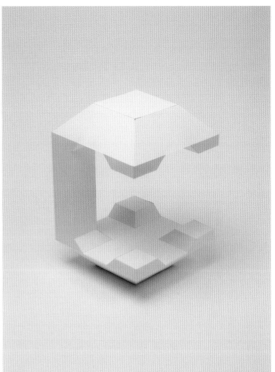

F for **4D Paper Lettering**

Four-dimensional alphabet lettering constructed with paper.
Each piece can be read from all four sides.

Design : LoSiento / Year : 2011

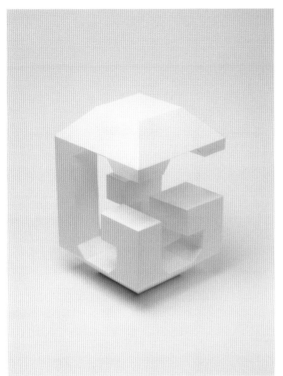

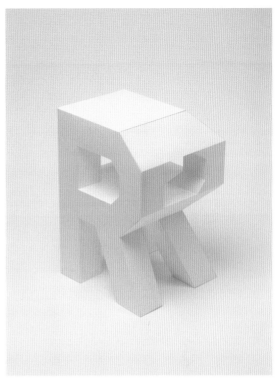

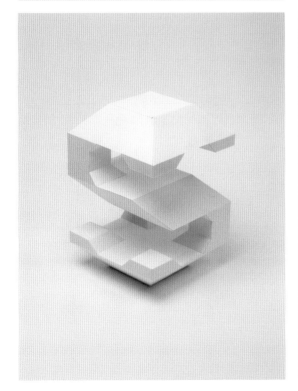

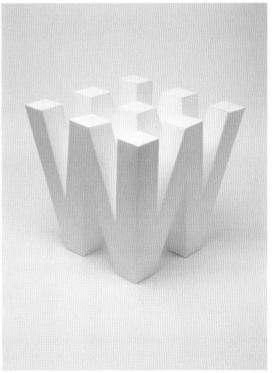

T for
Two Experiments

Two Experiments was set to express the beauty of hiragana
with texture and light, other than just the "outline" which
remains in print. Characters were crafted out of layered
paper using 3D data and model-building technique.

Design : Taku Satoh Design Office Inc. / Photography : Satoshi Askawa /
Client : Gallery Kobo / Year : 2009

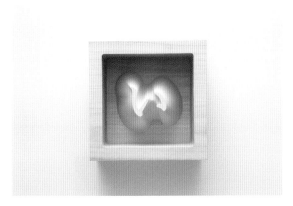

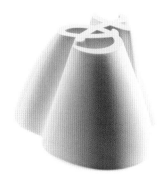

T for **TOFU**

Jean-Maxime Landry has difficulty finding this bean product interesting when he cooks, until tofu appears in bodies of letters like so they could communicate one day. TOFU is a student packaging work.

Design : Jean-Maxime Landry / Client : Packaging UQAM / Special Credits : Professor Sylvain Allard / Year : 2010

J for **Jobeur**

Nails packaging solution capitalising on the
head of nails to indicate the sizes and shapes
of the product on the packaging's surface.

Design : Pier-Phillipe Rioux / Client : Packaging
UQAM / Special Credits : Professor Sylvain Allard /
Year : 2010

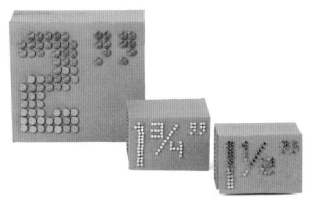

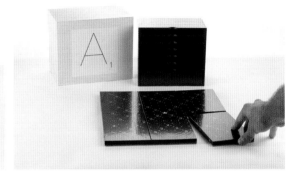

A for **A-1 Scrabble**

The designer edition of scrabble game with the notion to excite people about type design with tiles lettered in the typeface of users' choice or in assorted style. The scrabble boards are made of walnut lined with cork.

Design : Andrew Capener / Year : 2011

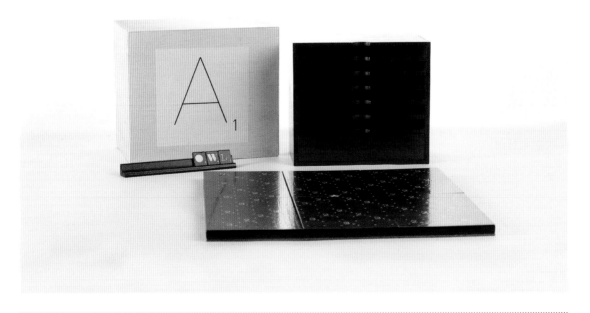

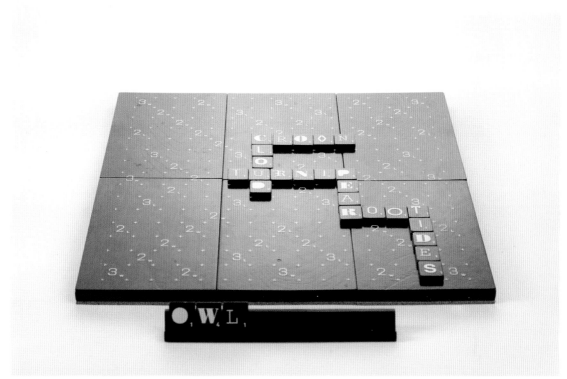

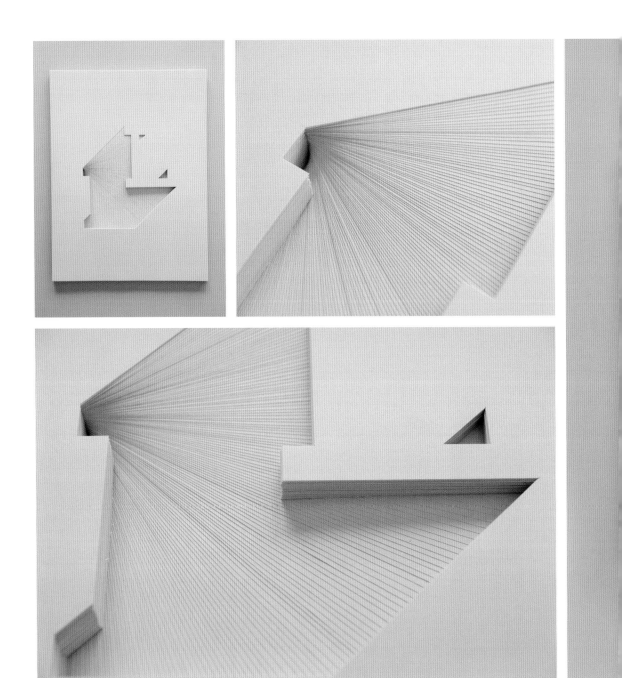

W for **White Types**

Typographic art pieces inspired by the subtlety of tone on tone
signage and the shadow play of three-dimensional letterforms. All
crafts were handplotted and cut out of multiple sheets of 80gsm
100% recycled paper.

Design : Bianca Chang / Year : 2011

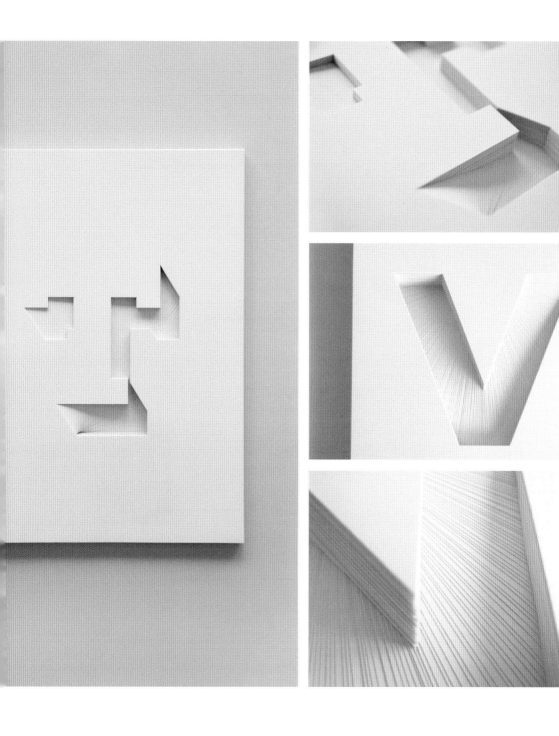

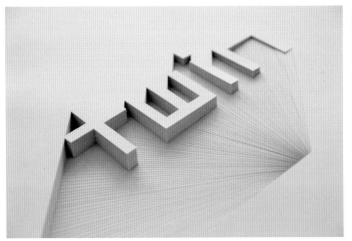
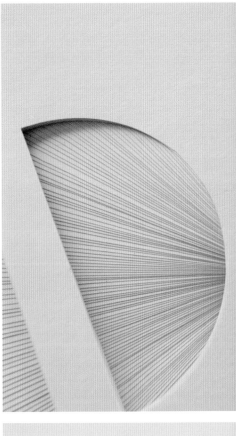
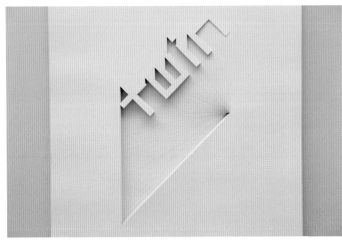

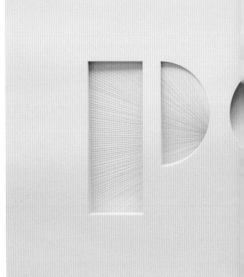

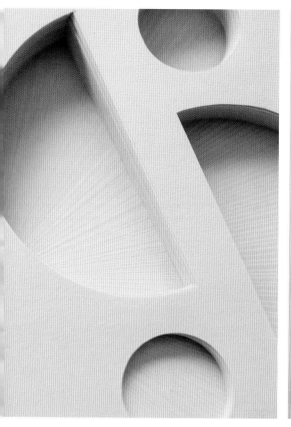

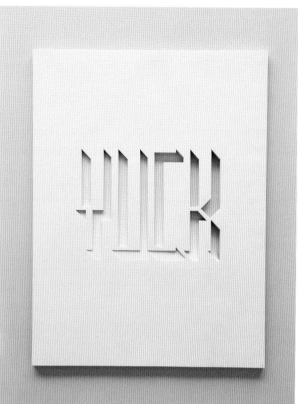

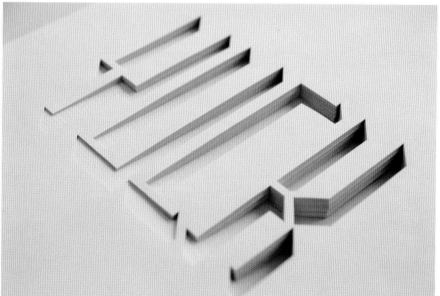

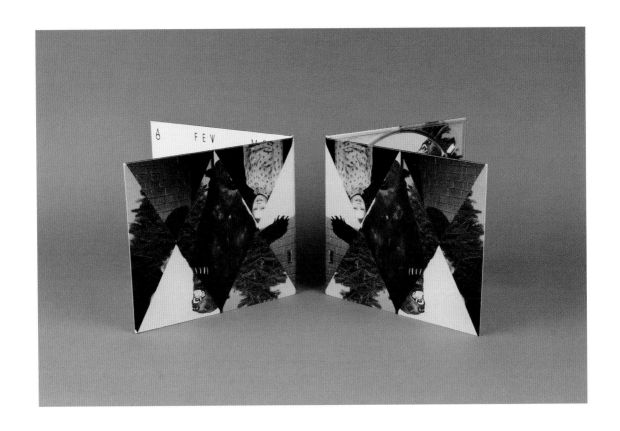

COZY SPHINX
WAVES QUART JUG
OF BAD MILK.

A for **A Few More Things**

Editorial and digipack design for DJ and producer Ivan Smagghe's new release.
The sleeve has adopted a pure pictorial approach on the front, with the disk's title
identified in custom typeface, Primary Shapes of Writing, on the inside.

Design : A is a name / Client : Ivan Smagghe / Year : 2011

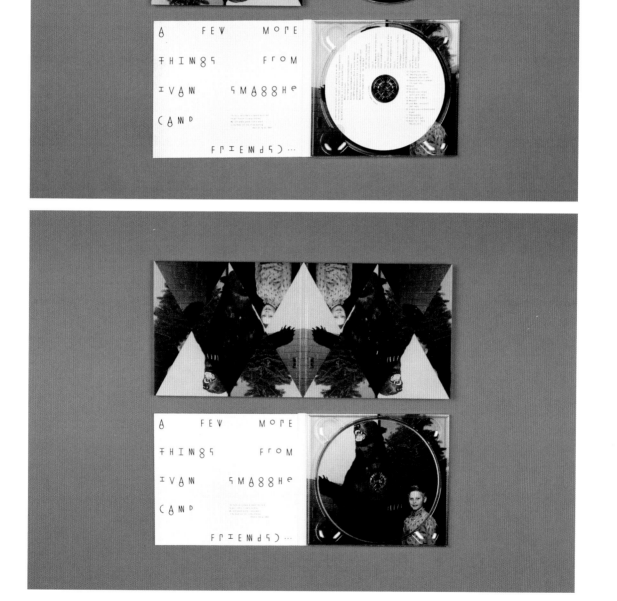

K U T S U

V for **Vuoden Huiput**

Identity based around "rebuses" to celebrate "Best of The Year" graphic design and advertising in Finland. The concept was to experiment with the relatively dubious nature of crowdsourcing and visual language imagined by internet users.

Design : Tsto Creative / Client : Grafia, Association of Professional Graphic Designers in Finland /
Web Application : Juhani Pelli / Year : 2011

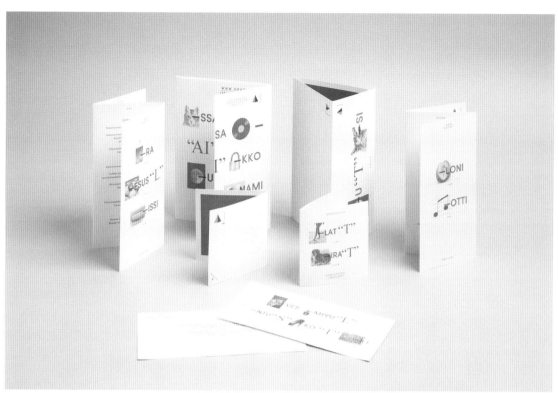

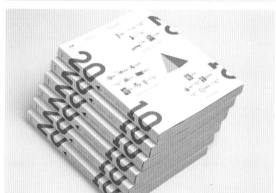

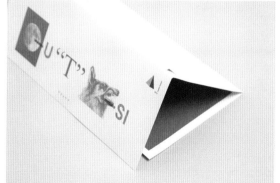

M for **Manna**

Cover design for Manna's third album, Shackles, with
elements of alternative rock and beautiful pop melodies.

Design : Tsto Creative / Photography : Knotan / Client : Sony Music,
Finland / Illustrations : Minni Havas / Year : 2011

W for
We are Helsinki

We Are Helsinki is a free bimonthly city magazine circulated around Helsinki. The periodical was designed afresh with new content and sections on city living and Finnish design accomplishments happening around the world.

Design : Tsto Creative / Client : We Are Publications / Year : 2009-

VIDEOCLUB

TOUR · 2011

DELTA
AMACURO

HAMBURG	16.09	ASTRA-STUBE
KÖLN	17.09	LIMES
HANNOVER	18.09	BÉI CHÉZ HEINZ
BREMEN	20.09	ZOLLKANTINE
JENA	21.09	ROSENKELLER
BERLIN	22.09	LEVEE
OFFENBACH	24.09	HAFEN 2

WWW
THISISTHEVIDEOCLUB
NET

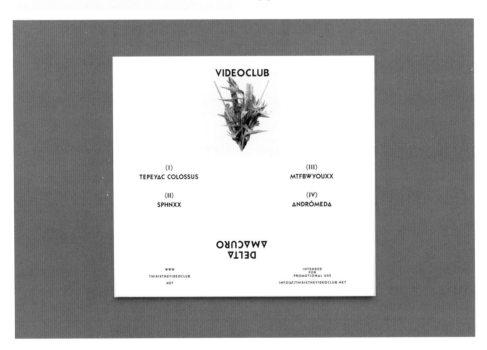

V for
Videoclub Delta Amacuro

A colourful reinterpretation of Videoclub's existing visual identity for their Delta Amacuro Tour 2011. The new solution has eliminated the cold, geometric shape and introduced a vibrant visual language reflecting their eclectic sound.

Design : HelloMe / Client : Videoclub / Flower Arrangements : Marsano / Year : 2011

VIDEOCLUB

TOUR   2011

ORUƆAMA
DELTA

WWW·THISISTHEVIDEOCLUB·NET

The Beatles *The End*

M for
Music Philosophy

Typographic interpretation of philosophical song quotes
produced in print and digitally for electronic devices.

Design : Mico Toledo / Year : 2011

BEST THINGS *come* FROM NOWHERE

Coldplay Speed of Sound

FOREVER MAY NOT BE -LONG- ENOUGH

Live Forever May Not Be Long Enough

TIME DON'T LET IT SLIP AWAY RAISE YOUR DRINKING GLASS HERE'S TO YESTERDAY

Aerosmith Full Circle

LIFE IS WHAT HAPPENS TO YOU WHILE YOU'RE BUSY MAKING OTHER PLANS

YOU CAN'T ALWAYS GET WHAT YOU WANT but if you try sometimes YOU JUST MIGHT FIND (YOU GET WHAT YOU) NEED

Rolling Stones You Can't Always Get What You Want

ALL YOU TOUCH AND ALL YOU SEE *is all* YOUR LIFE WILL EVER BE

Pink Floyd Breathe

IF YOU WANT TO MAKE THE WORLD A BETTER PLACE TAKE A LOOK AT YOURSELF {AND MAKE THE} CHANGE

Michael Jackson Man In The Mirror

DON'T LOSE THE DREAMS (INSIDE YOUR HEAD) THEY WILL ONLY BE THERE TILL → YOU ← ARE DEAD

Dave Matthews Band You Never Know

LOVE IS ALL YOU NEED

The Beatles All You Need Is Love

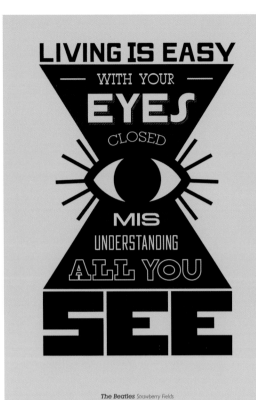

LIVING IS EASY
WITH YOUR
EYES
CLOSED
MIS
UNDERSTANDING
ALL YOU
SEE

The Beatles Strawberry Fields

I DON'T SEE
WHAT ANYONE CAN
SEE
IN ANYONE ELSE
but you

The Moldy Peaches Anyone Else But You

ALL
I CAN SAY
IS THAT
MY LIFE IS
PRETTY
PLAIN

Blind Melon No Rain

TOGETHER
WE
STAND
DIVIDED
WE
FALL

Pink Floyd Hey You

THE
SIMPLE
THINGS
YOU SEE
are all
COMPLICATED

The Who Substitute

IT'S A
BEAU
TIFUL
DAY
DON'T LET IT
GET AWAY

U2 Beautiful Day

WHEN I GO
FORWARDS
YOU GO
BACKWARDS
AND SOMEWHERE
WE WILL MEET

Radiohead Electioneering

YOU
LOVE
UNTIL YOU
DON'T

Regina Spektor On The Radio

P for **Playtype™**

A place where typography can be experienced by the public in space and through products and events. All tangible products are emblazoned with graphic characters and other type paraphernalia in coordination with the Playtype™ concept.

Design : e-Types / Photography : Enok Holsegaard, Lasse Bech Martinussen / Year : 2010

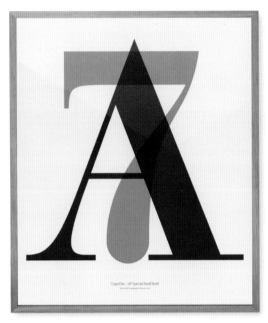

Typed in—JP Special Serif Bold

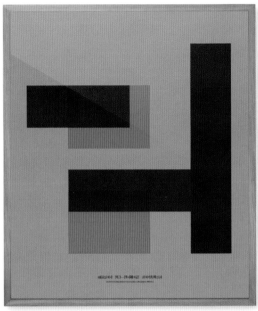

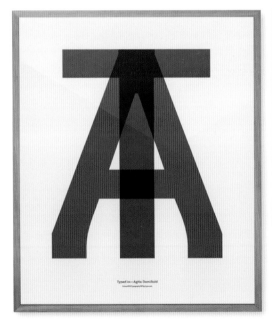

Typed in—Agita DemiBold

Typed in—Italian Plon Sport Light

1 Poster ABCD
2 Poster GREY

On facing page:
Poster A7, AE, AT, AG

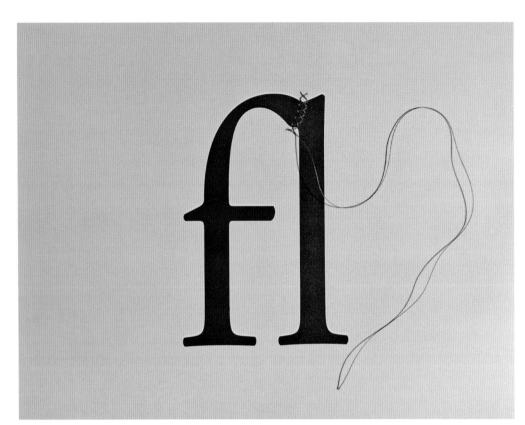

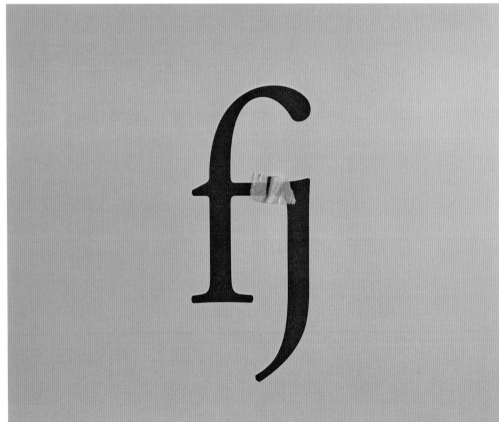

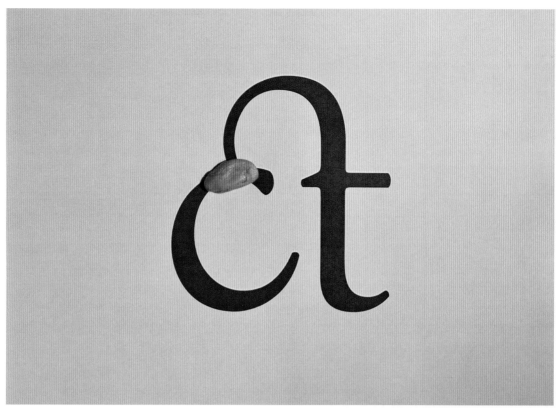

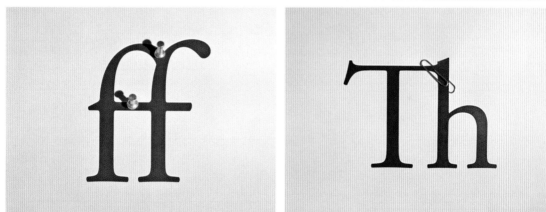

H for
How to Make
a Ligature

A real-world instance of how typographic ligatures
can actually be made. The joining point between
two graphemes were deliberately stylised with found
objects, such as gums, stitches and pins.

Design : David Schwen / Year : 2011

Bun
Lettuce
Tomato
Cheese
Beef
Onions
Bun

T for
Type Sandwiches

Type Sandwiches literally introduces sandwich recipes of
various origin with a refreshing twist. The collection
includes hamburger, grilled cheese sandwich, Chicago Dog,
cheesesteak, Cubano, s'more and taco.

Design : David Schwen / Year : 2009-11

Toast
Bacon
Lettuce
Tomato
Toast

Butter
Bread
Cheese
Bread
Butter

Bun
Mustard
Pickle
Peppers
Piccalilli

Onions
Frankfurter
Bun

Roll
Cheese
Steak
Onions
Roll

F for **Frame B**

'B' is for 'barbecue', where clients and partners gather for networking, fun and sharing views. The letter was made with kindling with blue and red facets to give a purple tone, the colour of Factum Finance's logotype.

Design : Zim&Zou / Client : Factum Finance / Year : 2011

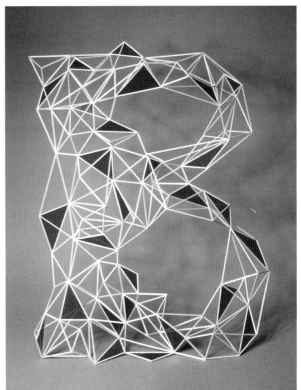

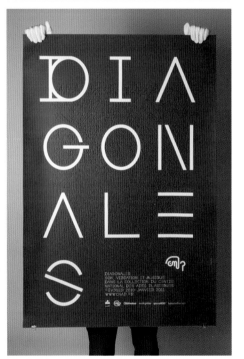

K for **Kenaki,**
La Grosse Basse

Posters for national acoustic art event, Diagonales, and outdoor electro
music festival, ME002. Digital typeface, Kenaki, and expanding foam
letters, La grosse basse, were custom-made for the events.

Design : Akatre / Client : Cnap, Mercredi Production / Year : 2010-11

P for
Pavillon Blanc

Pavillon Blanc is a media library and a center of
contemporary art. Named La Pavillon, the typeface was
created as the core component to characterise the place
with a link to its architectural design.

Design : Akatre / Client : City of Colomiers / Year : 2011

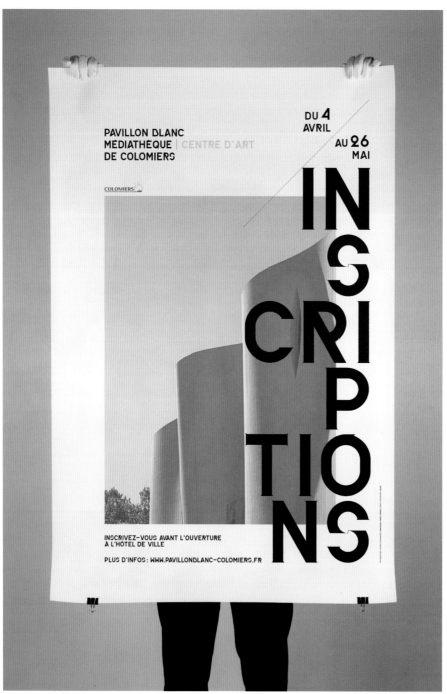

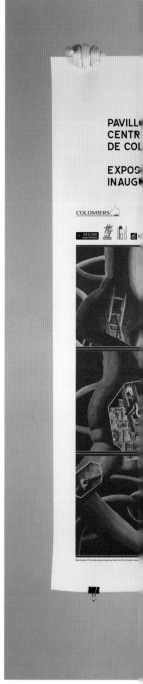

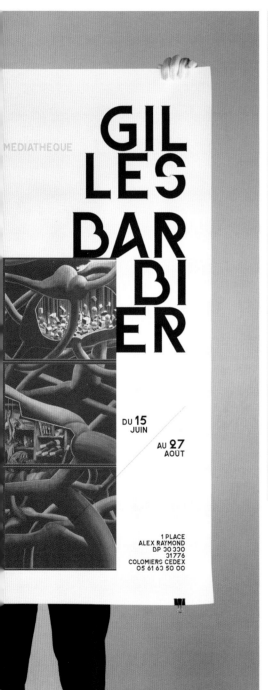

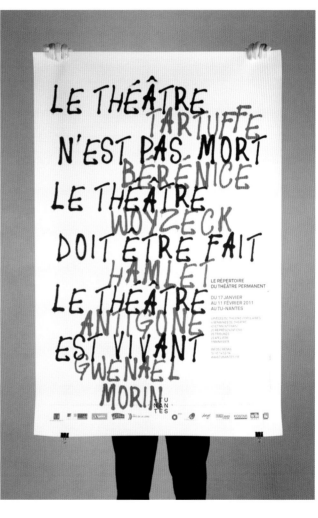

F for **Fun Festival 17**

Posters for TU Nantes' Festival Universitaire de Nantes, where
university students gather to introduce their work and public forums
are held. The elements of 'speech' and 'imperfections' have been
imparted in the modified letterforms, as a new typeface, Souffle.

Design : Akatre / Client : TU Nantes / Year : 2009-11

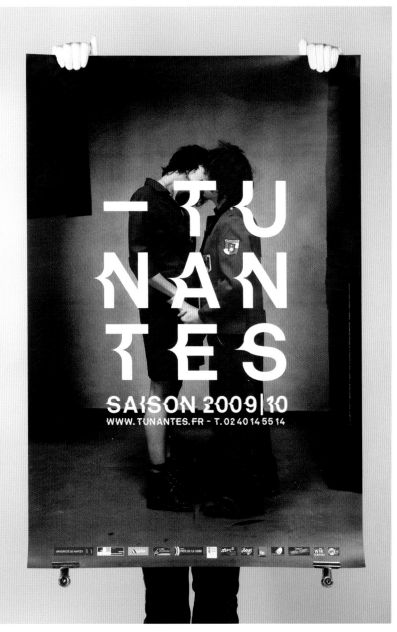

M for
Magali Jeambrun
Portfolio

A photographic series produced for French product designer, Magali Jeambrun's portfolio.

Design : A is a name / Client : Magali Jeambrun /
Special credits : Véronique Pêcheux / Year : 2009

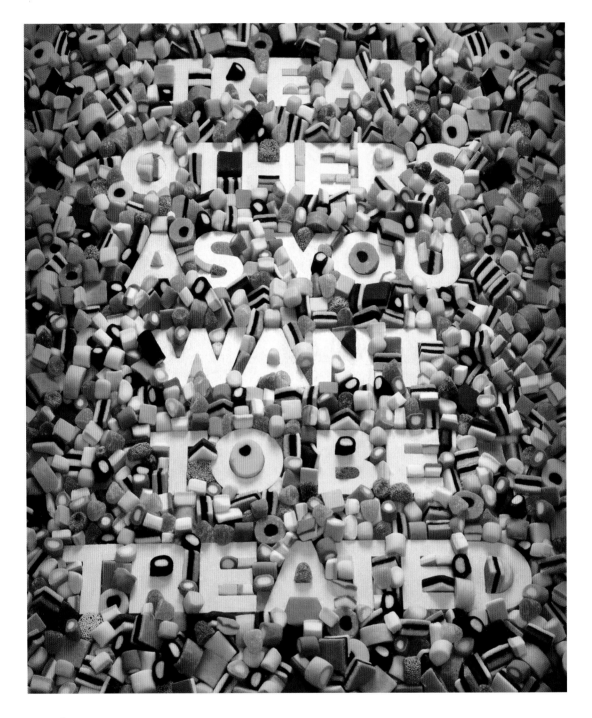

N for
New(er) Testaments

A typographical exploration summarising the demise of religion within the UK. While many of those practical wisdom seem to have lost their connection with time, selective phrases are graphically re-imagined to associate with modern life.

Design : Chris Nixon / Year : 2011

FOTO NAARDEN
FESTIVAL 2011

LET'S FACE IT
PORTRAITS OF DUTCH PHOTOGRAPHY

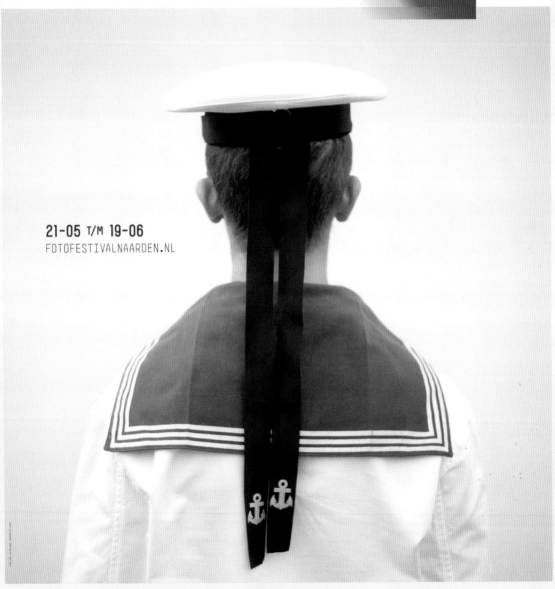

21-05 T/M 19-06
FOTOFESTIVALNAARDEN.NL

F for **FotoFest Naarden**

A small but flexible identity for a biannual photo festival themed 'Let's face it –
portraits of Dutch photography'. The logo and typographic variations have responded
to the idea with the event's initials presented as photographed stencil types.

Design : me studio / Client : Stichting FotoFestival, Naarden / Year : 2011

S for **Sculptural Types**

Experimental and commissioned work researching into sculptural forms and colour combinations in types with the use of paper.

Design : Jerome Corgier / Year : 2008-11

PaperDropCap for *The New York Times Style* Magazine based on 'Times'

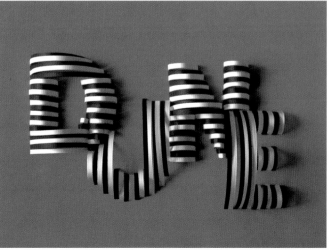

T for
The College Issue

Type treatment using stationery and textbook to illustrate
the theme of 'school' and 'studies' for *The New York Times'*
The College Issue.

Design : Eric Ku / Client : The New York Times / Year : 2008

C for
CHAIR/CHAIR

Chair built to redefine the object the word 'chair'
connotes. The inspiration was drawn from Joseph Kosuth's
One and Three Chair.

Design : Eric Ku / Year : 2009

S for **Sausage Type**

A personal project initiated to marry two of the designer's
personal favourites, sausages and typography.

Design : Martin Nicolausson / Year : 2009

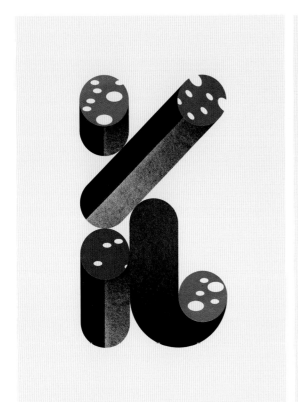

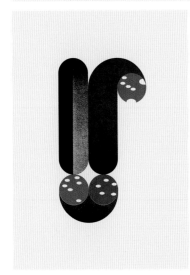

LIKE GRAMMAR, DESKTOP PUBLISHING HAS RULES— BREAK THEM AND YOU SUFFER.

1 Don't Sweat my Swag / Nike / 2010
2 Hell Yeah / Personal / 2010
3 May the Force / Colher / 2011
4 Mortar&Pestle / Mortar&Pestle / 2011

On facing page:
5 Support Japan / Wall for Japan / 2011

V for
Vector Lettering

A collection of vector-based typographic illustrations expressing personal aspirations and messages on apparels, publications and background decoration for electronic devices' screens.

Design : André Beato

W for **Write A Bike**

A bike series imagined to be personalised with the bike owner's own name physically installed as the frame. Juri Zaech's goal is to build at least one of them and ride it through the streets of Paris.

Design : Juri Zaech / Year : 2011

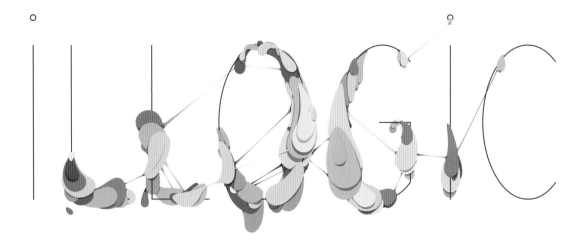

T for **Text-ure**

Headlines graphically playing on words' context to hint at the themes. *Illogic* was done for *GÖOO MAGAZINE* in random patches of semifluid colours. Underneath is the fusion of Nike and Foot Locker customised to celebrate the legendary AirMax 90.

Design : Superexpresso / Year : 2011

A for
Ai Records
10th Anniversary

Number 'ɪo' as a tangle of chubby elephants
messing up with mushrooms in a grey tone
with front and back versions designed for
album *WHEN I WAS TEN* for Ai Records' ɪoth
anniversary celebrations.

Design : Superexpresso /
Client : Area Info Records UK / Year : 2010

10 Nomi di città con la "F"

Falmouth - Stati Uniti
Ferreñafe - Perù
Fethiye - Turchia
Fohnsdorf - Austria
Foix - Francia
Folgaria - Italia
Fougamou - Gabon
Francoforte - Germania
Freetow - Sierra Leone
Funafuti - Tuvalu

Lingua parlata

Inglese
Spagnolo
Turco - Curdo - Dimli
Tedesco - Lingue regionali
Francese
Italiano
Francese - Lingue regionali
Tedesco
Inglese
Lingua tuvaluana

Designer

Federico Galvani - Happycentro

Città - Nazione d'origine

Verona - Italia

Lingua parlata

Italiano

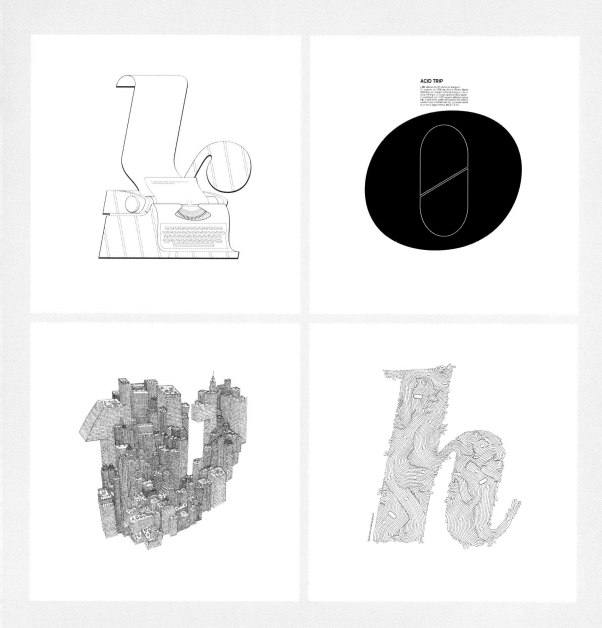

A for **Alphaposter**

With the concept built around "travelling", alphabets were picked and stylised, along with ten cities whose names begin with the letter and the languages their people speak. Designed in collaboration with design community, Scalacolore.

Design : Happycentro / Special Credits : Giuliano Garonzi / Year : 2008

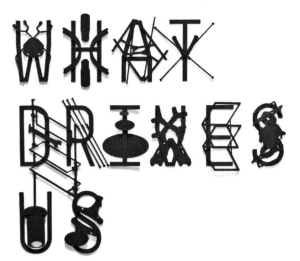

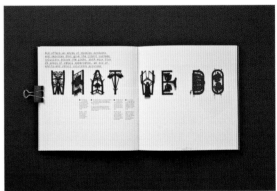

 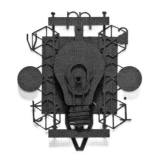 

A for
ALU Company Book

ALU specialises in modular merchandising systems, and Happycentro
wanted to explain their values in a series of keywords. Modular
elements were initially produced as paper cuts before piecing together
as types and artworks for ALU's visual identity and company book.

Design : Happycentro / Client : ALU / Year : 2011

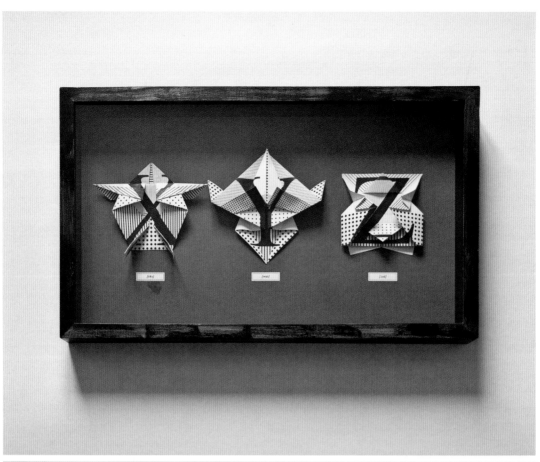

T for **Typografly**

Letters interpreted as specimens identified by phonetic
notations beneath. The letters were a response to Gallery
Nucleus's exhibition held to celebrate handdrawn
letterforms and experimental typography.

Design : Happycentro / Special Credits : Alexis Kaneshiro / Year : 2011

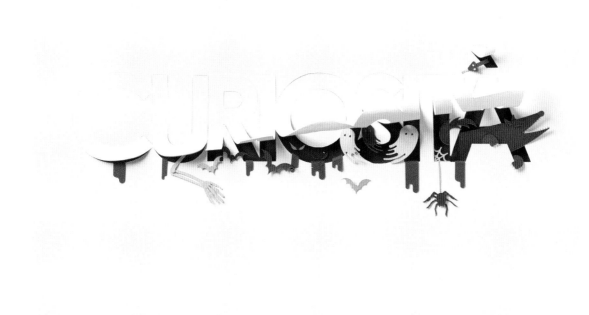

I for **Intelligence In Lifestyle**

Custom-designed titles to introduce the monthly theme of column "Remo Contro"
contributed by Italian philosopher, Remo Bodei. Context can be traced throughout
the artwork from its materials and the subjects they depict.

Creative Direction : Francesco Franchi / Design : Happycentro / Client : Il Sole 24 Ore / Year : 2011

V for **VITA**

Crafted letters depicting human's anatomy to illustrate
a monthly feature's theme on "Vita (life)". The column
is contributed by Italian philosopher, Remo Bodei to
Intelligence In Lifestyle magazine.

Creative Direction : Francesco Franchi / Design : Happycentro /
Client : Il Sole 24 Ore / Year : 2011

Mozambique, officially the Republic of Mozambique (Portuguese: Moçambique or República de Moçambique), is a country in southeastern Africa bordered by the Indian Ocean to the east, Tanzania to the north, Malawi and Zambia to the northwest, Zimbabwe to the west and Swaziland and South Africa to the southwest. It was explored by Vasco da Gama in 1498 and colonized by Portugal in 1505. By 1510, the Portuguese had virtual control of all of the former Swahili sultanates on the east African coast. From about 1500, Portuguese trading posts and forts became regular ports of call on the new route to the east. Mozambique became independent in 1975, to which it became the People's Republic of Mozambique shortly after, and was the scene of an intense civil war from 1977 to 1992. The country is a member of the Community of Portuguese Language Countries and the Commonwealth of Nations and an observer of the Francophonie. Mozambique (Moçambique) was named by the Portuguese after Msumbiji, the Swahili name of Mozambique Island and port-town. Mozambique's life expectancy and infant mortality rates are both among the worst ranked in the world. Its Human Development Index is one of the lowest on earth.

Wikipedia – The Free Encyclopedia
Federico Galvani – Happycentro – Italy – 2009
Photography by Federico Padovani

T for **Toy Soldier**

Poster designed to imagine children's everyday life in
Mozambique surrounded by conflicts, bullets and blood.
For a fund-raising art show organised by ASEM.

Design : Happycentro / Special Credits : Jamie N Kim, Mo Manager,
Wieden+Kennedy / Year : 2009

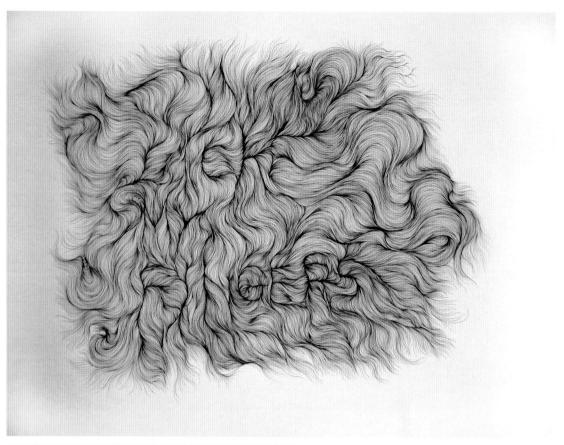

O for **Organs (Dessin)**

Organs (Dessin) is a collection of large scale drawings created to explore the legibility of text where letters intertwine like organic matters. The piece aims to connect viewers to something that are both alive and dead, and are often disconcerting.

Design : Julie Morel / Year : 2008-09

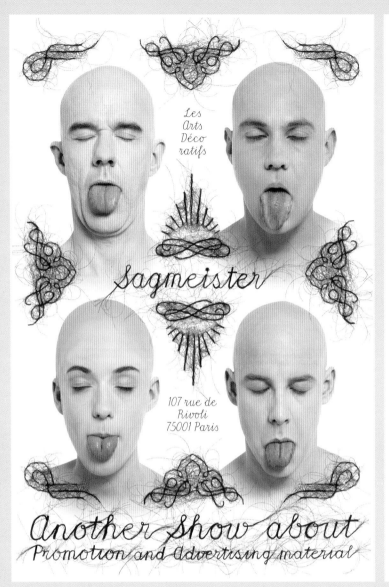

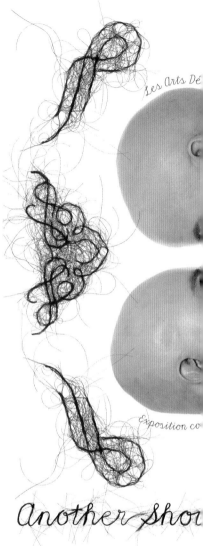

L for
Les Arts Décoratifs

Promotional poster for Sagmeister Inc's exhibition at Les Arts
Décoratifs in Paris. The Sagmeister team had shaved their heads and
thus the idea of "weaving" types out of real hair, from Jessica Walsh.

Art Direction : Stefan Sagmeister / Design : Jessica Walsh / Photography : Henry
Hargreaves / Hair Art : Kerry Howley / Makeup : Anastasia Durasaova / Year : 2011

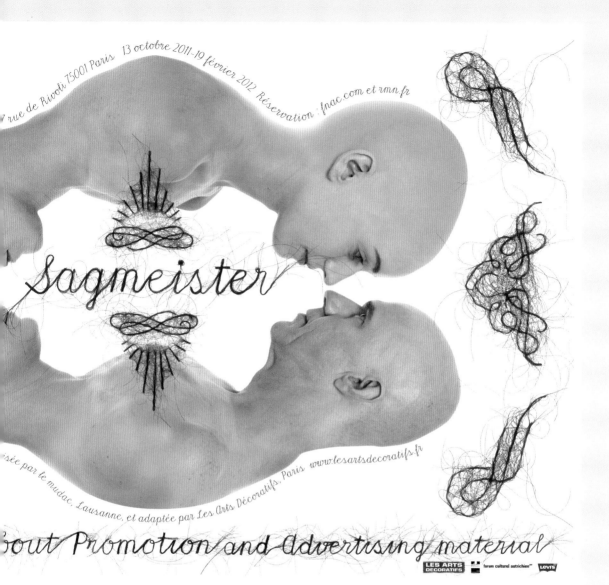

A for
Aizone FW11
Campaign

Typographic treatment for animated billboard
installed at Houston and Lafayette street in SoHo.

Art direction : Stefan Sagmeister / Design : Jessica Walsh /
Year : 2011

P for
People Love Music

People Love Music is an Oslo-based club concept that plays soul, disco and electro. Their visual identity celebrates the individual elements that reflect their core values in the name with numbers to bring out the joy of music and nightlife.

Design : Bureau Bruneau (Ludvig Bruneau Rossow) / Client : People Love Music /
Special Credits : Henrik Wold Kraglund / Year : 2010

E for **EXZEM**

Visual identity for HipHop musician Exzem based around
custom display typeface HM Extra. The type combines
metaphoric imageries that allude to backpack-HipHop clichés,
anonymity of coming from the countryside, the musician's
selfmade-approach and story of the album's name.

Design : HelloMe / Client : Tunnelblick Music / Year : 2011

TUNNELBLICK MUSIC PRESENTS
EXZEM
SCHREIBMASCHINE
WWW.EXZEM.ORG
WWW.TUNNELBLICK-MUSIC.DE

DEINE FREUNDIN

09:
Title: Deine Freundin feat. Mr. Knight
Text: F. Balush, D. Schomaker, D. Debbrick
Music: T. Jensen
Scratches: D. Freundin

ICH+HER

DU WUNDERST DICH

07:
Title: Du wunderst dich...
Text: D. Schomaker
Music: D. Dufenmeister
Music: D. Dufenmeister

GLEICH GÜLTIGKEIT

10:
Title: Gleichgültigkeit
Text: D. Dufenmeister
Music: D. Dufenmeister
Scratches: D. Schomaker

MEINE SACHE

01:
Title: Meine Sache (Intro)
Text: D. Dufenmeister
Music: C. Dufenmeister
Scratches: D. Schomaker

FEST STELLUNGEN

02:
Title: Feststellungen
Text: D. Schomaker
Music: D. Dufenmeister
Scratches: D. Schomaker

GENUG IST GENUG

06:
Title: Genug ist Genug
Text: D. Schomaker
Music: C. Dufenmeister
Blues Harp: M. Schöngel

NIGHT+DAY

04:
Title: Night+Day feat. Günna
Text: D. Schomaker, D. Tomczax
Music: B. Grissmp

M(A)(C)K

08:
Title: Magllick
Text: D. Schomaker
Music: D. Luhse
Scratches: D. Schomaker

IQ-RAP

05:
Title: Iq-Rap feat. Dos
Text: D. Schomaker
Music: D. Dufenmeister
Scratches: D. Schomaker

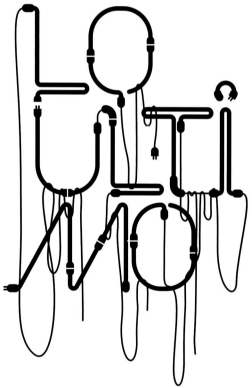

L for **Lo Ultimo**

Logotype developed as the new identity of Lo Ultimo, a
short programme of technology, trends and style for Sony
Entertainment Television in Latin America.

Design : Plenty / Client : Sony Entertainment / Year : 2010

E for
Evolution of Type

An anatomy of letters performed to authenticate Frederic W. Goudy's *The Alphabet and Elements of Lettering* (1918), which compared the invention and development of alphabets and writings to the coming of men.

Design : Andreas Scheiger /
Year : 2010-2011

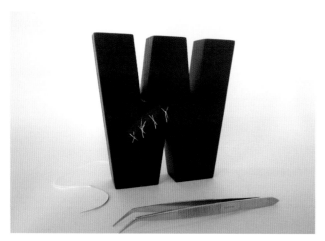

GABRIEL GARCÍA MÁRQUEZ ZWÖLF GESCHICHTEN AUS DER FREMDE

WILHELM BUSCH
BILDERGESCHICHTEN

E for
Evolution of Type,
Exhibit 16

As a matter of fact, metal types and letterpress prints are
fading away from modern day life, and this is perhaps how
they would turn up one day. All letters in this collection are
cut balsa wood cast in polyester glass casting resin.

Design : Andreas Scheiger / Year : 2011

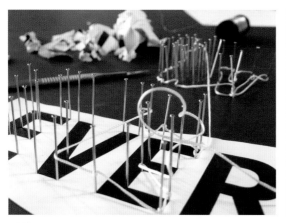
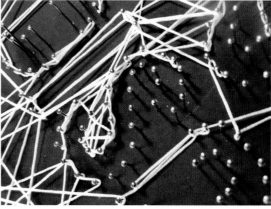
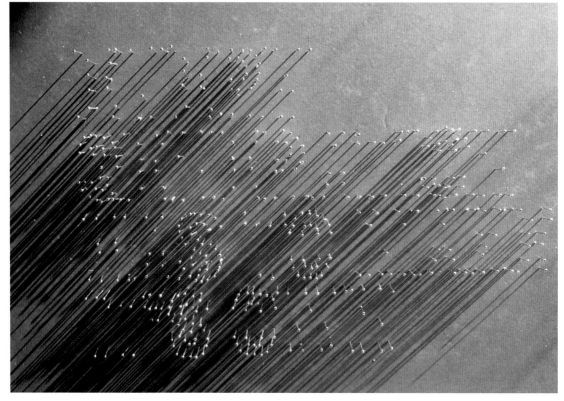

G for
Generations

A typographical poster illustrating one of the designer's
favourite quotes from Milton Glaser with threads and
steel pins. The composition is experimental in nature
but expressive of the idea behind the quotes.

Design : me studio / Year : 2010

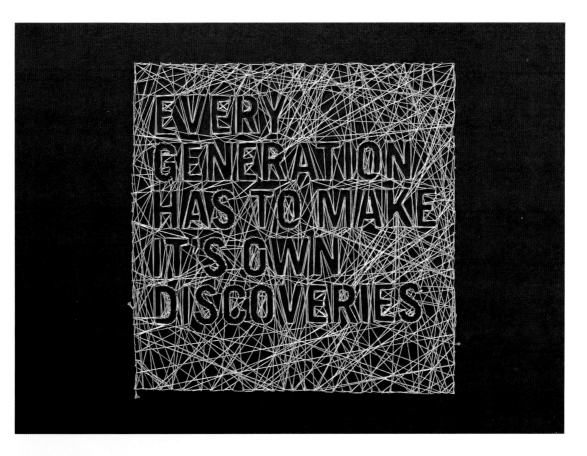

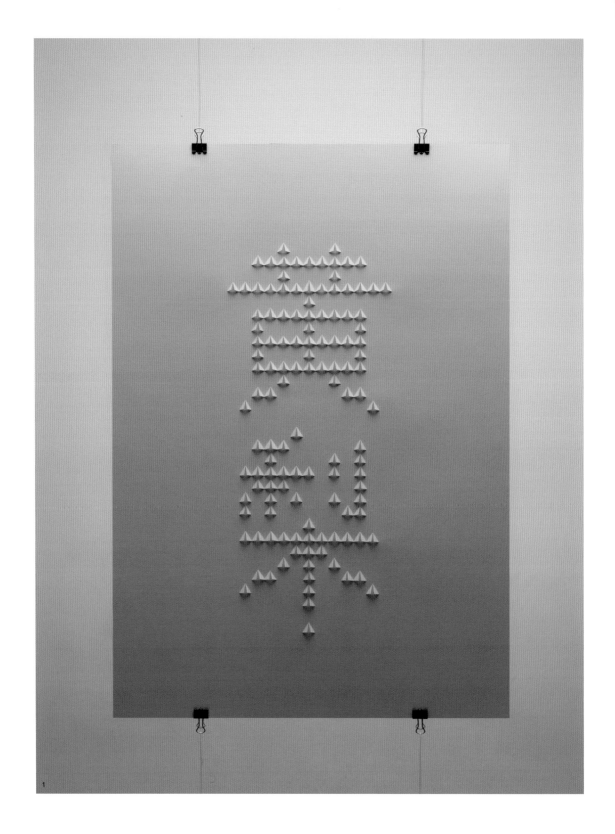

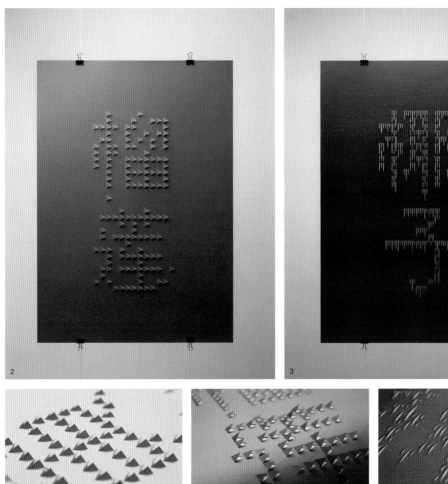

M for
Makanlah Buah-Buahan
Tempatan

Pineapples, durians and coconuts are the quintessential Malaysian fruits. The posters celebrate the fruits by their names and simple yet unique geometric features for an exhibition held in conjunction with KL Design Week. Each piece is meticulously crafted by hand.

Design : Roots / Client : Makanlah Buah-Buahan Tempatan / Year : 2011

1 Pineapple
2 Durian
3 Coconut

C for **Cocoon**

Handmade miniature developed for a story book based on a new recycled paper. The font adds up to a progressing evolution of life on a mini planet where leisure is accompanied by more vegetation at every phrase.

Design : Studiowill / Client : Antalis (HK) Ltd / Year : 2010

T for **'T' SHIRTS**

More than just a conceptual idea, 'T' shirts are wearable designs that embrace the distinguishable silhouettes of Helvetica, Caslon, Baskerville, Courier and Cooper Black. Shirt sizes are all indicated in point sizes – up to several thousands – on the tags.

Creative Direction : Masashi Kawamura / Design : Masashi Kawamura, Itaru Yonenaga / NO CONTROL AIR / Production : Itaru Yonenaga / NO CONTROL AIR / Makeup : Chichi Saito / Photography : Munetaka Tokuyama / Year : 2008-10

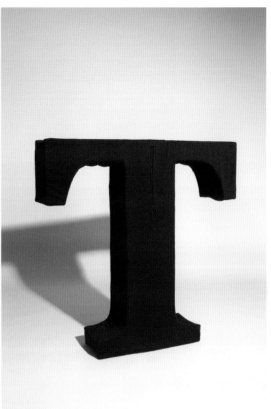

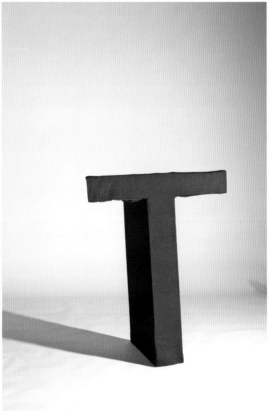

P for
Puma — The Games We Play

A global advertising campaign where Puma put up a play about "play" and sports inside its own name, measuring 60-foot tall, on a large soundstage. The activities going on around 'Puma' were shot to produce collateral and fashion lookbook for the brand.

Creative Direction: Alex Lowe / Design : National Forest Design / Video Direction : Jared Eberhardt / Photography : Jon Johnson / Client : Puma Sport Co. / Year : 2009

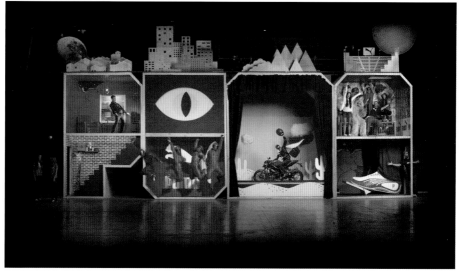

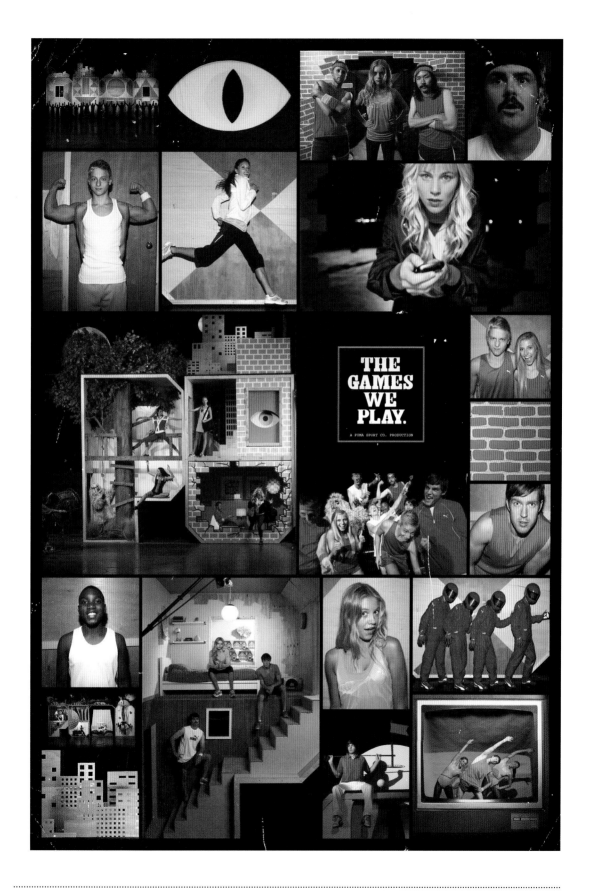

THE
GAMES
WE
PLAY.

A PUMA SPORT CO. PRODUCTION

Z for **Zygomatique**

'Zygomatique' is French for 'cheekbone'. The specialised term was made explicit as
arranged as a showcase of human body parts, manually created by modelling clay.

Design : Plasticbionic / Photography : Paloma Rincón / Client : Serial Cut™ / Year : 2009

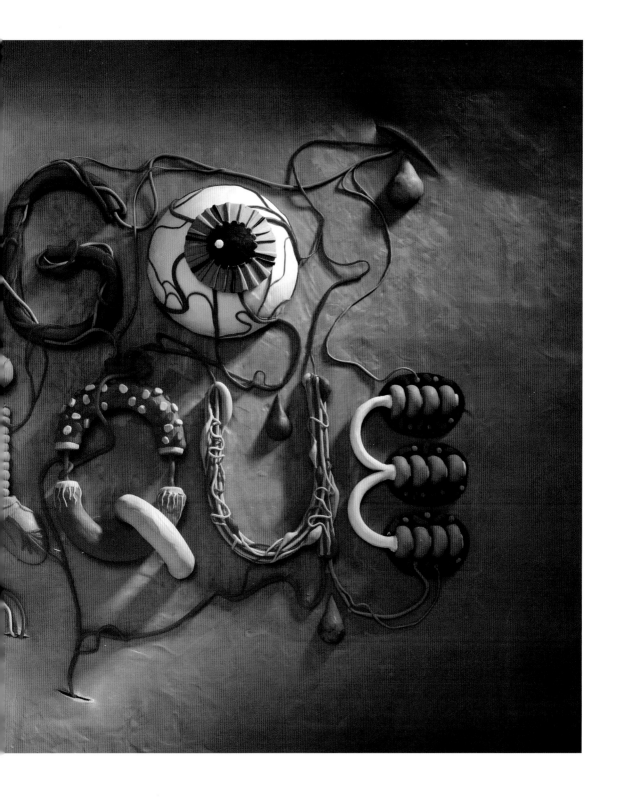

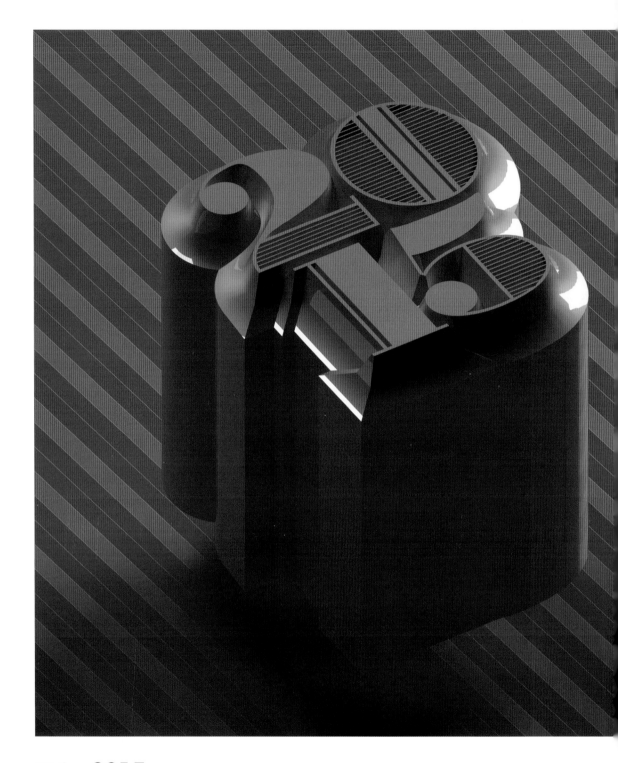

T for **2015**

Originated by (RED), the year 2015 is set to be the end of mother-to-child HIV transmission and start of the aids-free generation. In support of this goal, artists come together to interpret the number 2015. This is Plasticbionic's vision of 2015.

Design : Plasticbionic / Client : Serial Cut™ / Year : 2009

S for
Spanish Ham Roll

An image to promote Spanish design in the UK, showcasing the letter 'S' made from parma ham. The image has been published in ICEX's annual magazine, *Diseño*.

Design : Serial Cut™, Jimmy Andersson / Client : ICEX / Year : 2010

T for **THE COLORS**

Promotional campaign highlights the new paint product range brought by Jotun. Splashes of paint were added to set off the statement with an opulent colour appeal.

Design : Serial Cut™ / Photography : Paloma Rincón / Client : Jotun / Year : 2011

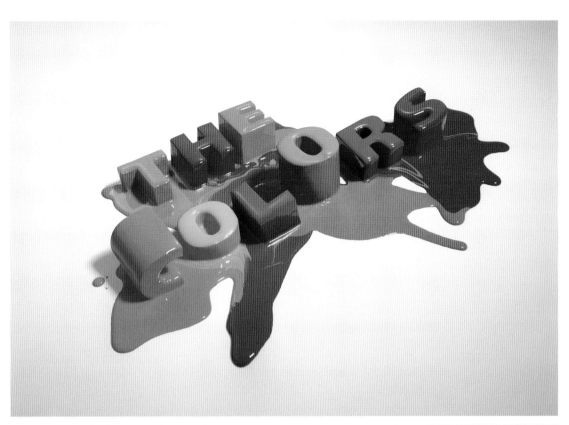

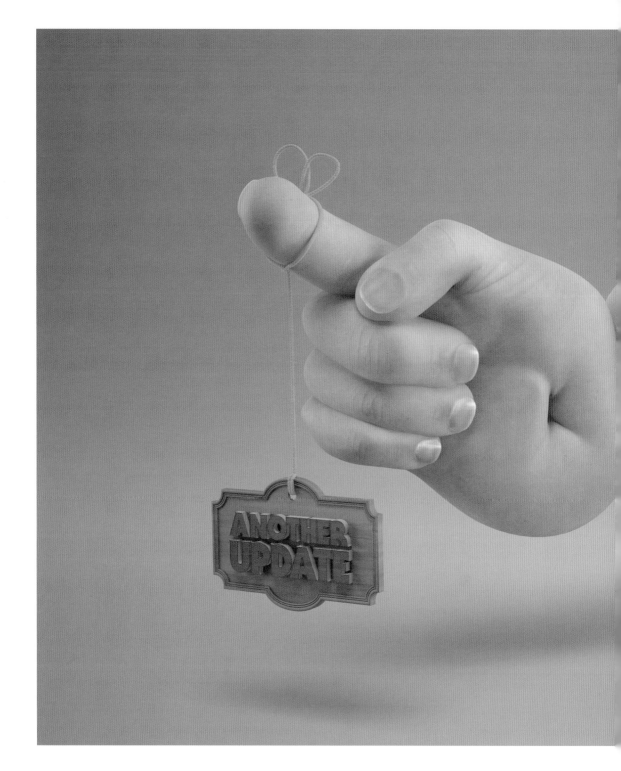

O for **Oops!**

A artwork inspired by a 1970s painting and made to point the studio's
portfolio updates lightheartedly on their website.

Design : Serial Cut™, Jimmy Andersson / Year : 2010

W for **Wakeboarding**

Three humourous allusions to wakeboarding with references to bible stories and daily life facts. The project was accomplished in collaboration with Curt Detweiler.

Design : Plasticbionic / Year : 2010

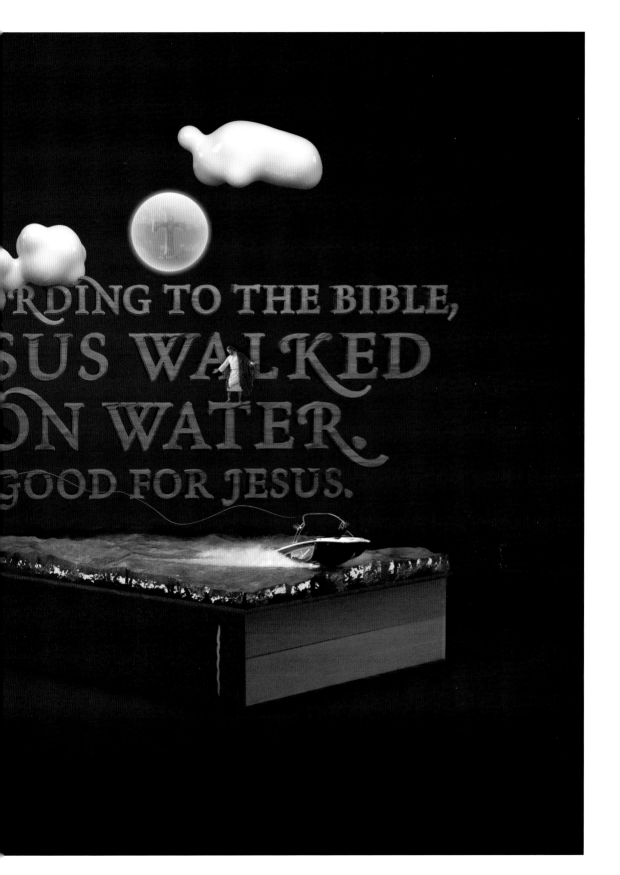

F for **Flexipop**

Customised types created as an homage to the great
name of Flexipop, a New Wave music compilation
from the 1980s.

Design : Plasticbionic / Client : Serial Cut™ / Year : 2009

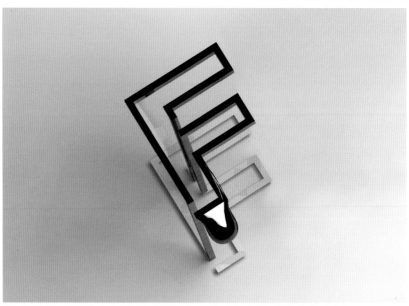

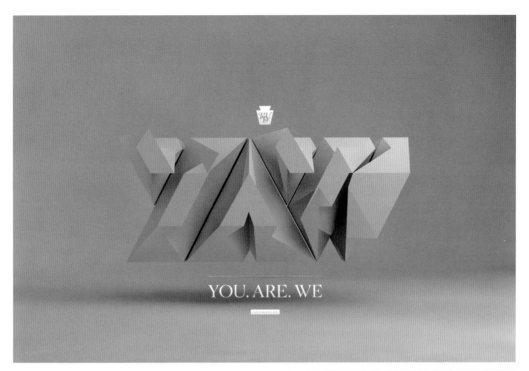

YOU. ARE. WE

Y for **YOU.ARE.WE**

Illustration and typographical treatment,
depicting "YAW", for the You Are We project.

Design : Plasticbionic / Client : KDU / Year : 2010

I for
Icon & It's So Hard

Promotional projects to express ideas within its own words. *Icon* pays
homage to emoticons with Japanese rubber and jelly beans. *It's So Hard*
pokes fun at life with jelly blocks made in hands with Mr. Oso.

Design : Serial Cut™, Kristian Touborg / Photography : Paloma Rincón / Year : 2011

D for **Druggercoasters**

Alcohol, cocaine and xtacy are the most common problems in Spain.
The anti-drug advertisement series was made to publicise the message,
"You know where the fun part begins, but not where it will end".

Design : Serial Cut™, Jimmy Andersson / Client : FAD / Year : 2011

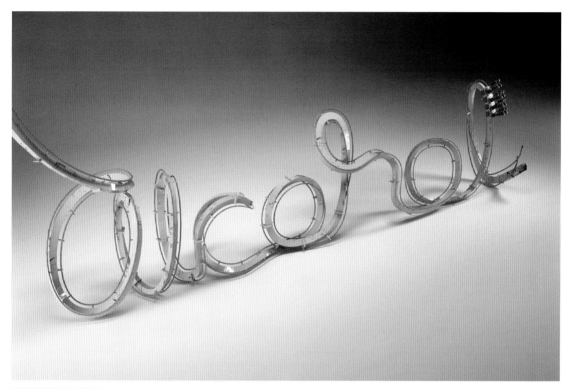

S for **Steve Back**

A fun and bouncy logo for Steve Back. The brief was to make Back's name fun and thus, the inflatable castle in which everybody would wish to jump.

Design : Toby And Pete / Client : Steve Back / Year : 2010

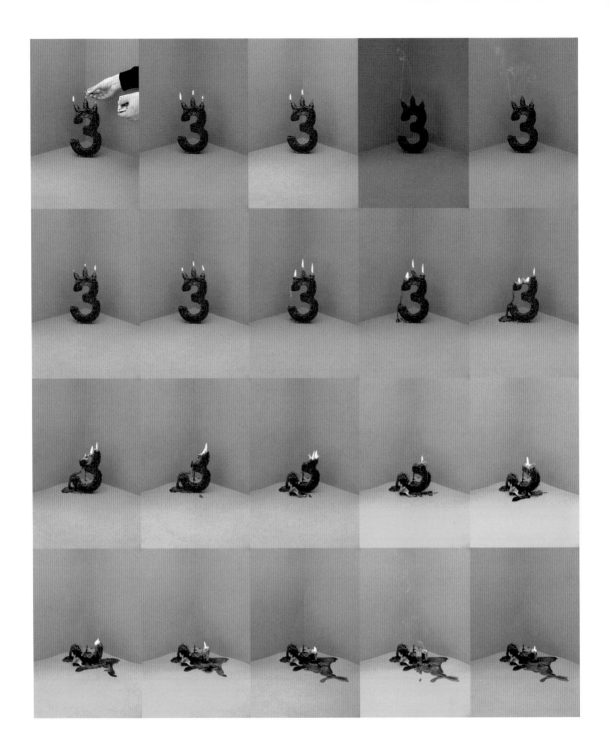

F for **Fragil 3 Years**

Illustrations and poster for Fragil's third birthday party. The design has captured a triple '3' – the digit, number of wax candles and flames – dissolving to resonate with its name and celebrate the event.

Design : Plasticbionic / Photography : Souenellen / Client : Fragil Musique / Year : 2010

FRAGIL
★★★
Les 3 ans

NANTES
20H00 > 10H00

SAMEDI 16 AVRIL 2011

DOUBLEDECKER *FRAGIL NANTES*
SPROG aka GORMAK *WBA NANTES*
JANKOLA *VISIT VISIT NANTES*
DARABI *GET THE CURSE NANTES*
MIKHAIL *GET THE CURSE PARIS*

MYAKO *MARTIAL FUNK - CONFORTZONE PARIS*
CLAYTON GUIFFORD *FRAGIL PARIS*
CEDRIC BORGHI *FRAGIL - LIVE ! NANTES*
MIKAEL COSTANTINI *FRAGIL NANTES*
RAPHAËL *FRAGIL NANTES*

20H00 - 00H00
ABSENCE
6 quai François Mitterrand,
44200 Nantes

00H00 - 7H00
CASTEL CLUB
13 rue Mathelin Rodier,
44000 Nantes

7H00 - AFTER
ABSENCE

 facebook.com/fragil.party   vimeo.com/fragilparty   myspace.com/fragilmusique

I'M NOT LIKE A HELVETICA
I'M JUST A FREAK

L for
Liquid Type in Motion

The beauty of this font was in motion, fluidity and evanescence. Ruslan Khasanov's idea was to show how fleeting and fragile the ink letters are when exposed to water. The letters appear and disperse, like a bizarre dance of life, between birth and death.

Design : Ruslan Khasanov / Year : 2011

L for **Love for Words**

Collaborative artworks where Pomme Chan composed the
illustrations and Sean Freeman experimented with the drawings to
create the different typographic artwork. *All You Need Is Love* was
later exhibited at a design festival in Bangkok.

Design : There Is / Illustrations : Pomme Chan / Year : 2010-11

The **▮**
with Jus**▮**

Ap**▮**
Ca**▮**
Gra**▮**

Art**▮**

T for **The Decemberists**

Sean Freeman's first gig poster for The Decemberists' show depicts the band's name configured with a bunch of twigs to suggest their music character and as an interesting challenge at the same time.

Design : There Is / Client : The Decemberists / Red Light Management / Year : 2011

ists
s Earle

11
ge
MI

man

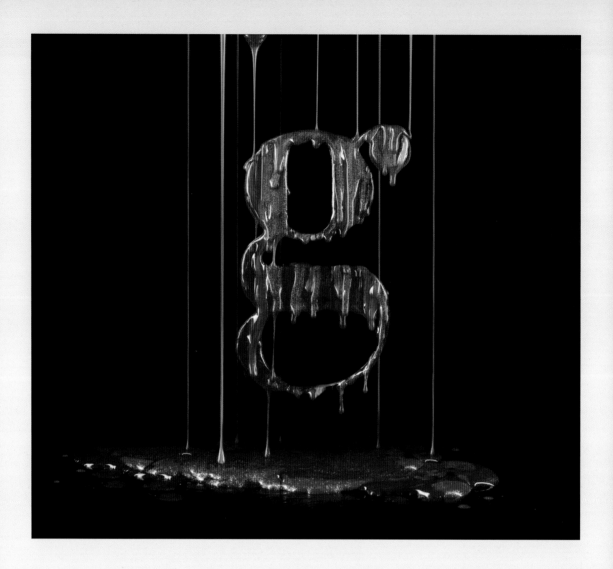

D for
__Dip & Drip__

Types custom-made as cover art for *Computer Arts'* typography issue and invitation to Cream, an international graduation show of 20 art director and copywriter teams. On this page is a Bodoni 'g' dipped in nail varnish, and cream lettering on the next.

Design : There Is / Client : Computor Arts, The Talent Business / Year : 2009-10

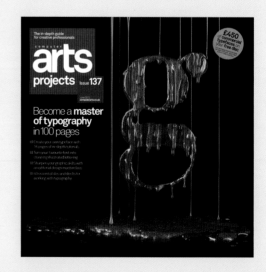

F for **Fear & Suisse**

Type treatment rendered with dynamic effects. *Fear* is a headline
artwork for *Wired* magazine that imitates a breaking glass bottle.
Suisse depicts the designer's friend's design studio in milk splashes.

Design : There Is / Year : 2009-10

D for
Digital Temple

Artwork as chapter dividers for online magazine *Digital Temple* created with an open brief. Sean Freeman was responsible for the treatment to the lettering and the finish and his brother, Karl Freeman, had worked on the processing.

Design : There Is / Processing : Karl Freeman /
Client : Digital Temple / Year : 2011

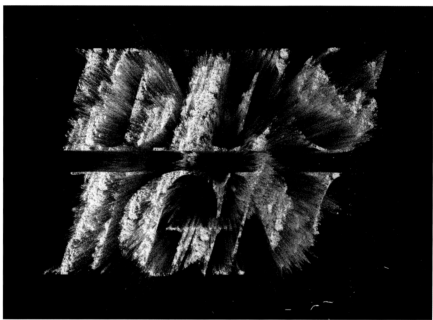

T for
Typography in Water

This is one of the ways YouWorkForThem experiment with types. Instead of looking up and posting new fonts, they picked five of their most popular fonts from their collection. This is what they become different under water.

Design : YouWorkForThem / Year : 2010

Y for
YCN — A is for Award

YCN has redesigned their trophies with an 'A' to bestow upon new creative excellence. Several letter 'A' models as a remark about the award, so as to reference designers' creative processes and the year's theme, The Element of Surprise.

Design : Julien Vallée / Photography : Simon Duhamel / Client : YCN / Year : 2009

O for
On Language

Custom-designed type for William Safire's column, On Language, in *The New York Times* magazine.

Design : Julien Vallée / Client : The New York Times / Year : 2010

L for
Love Is Cocaine —
Magnetism

Visual identity for Nu'Pop musician, Love Is Cocaine, based on their album, Magnetism. The idea of attraction is melded into an appealing darkness with infographics founding the artists' initials, LiC.

Design : HelloMe / Photography : Ramon Haindl / Client : Ground Records, Love Is Cocaine / Year : 2011

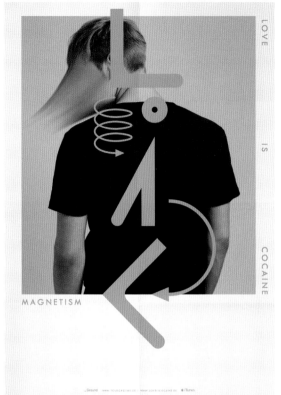

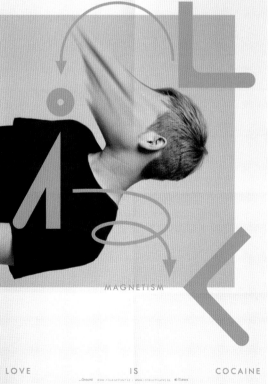

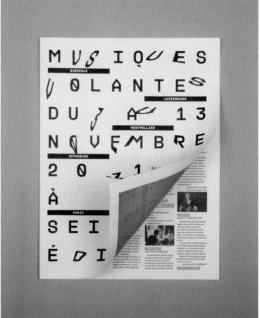

M for
Musiques Volantes

Musiques Volantes is an eclectic moment of contemporary music
based at Metz. A complete identity system stemmed in electronic
interference prevails the music festival's communication through
its custom typeface and digital edits in the images.

Design : A is a name / Client : Festival Musiques Volantes / Year : 2011

MUSIQUES VOLANTES

SEIZIÈME ÉDITION

À METZ

JEUDI 03 NOVEMBRE À 19H00
VERNISSAGE + CONCERTS
COPRODUCTION METZ EN SCÈNES ET MUSIQUES VOLANTES
LES TRINITAIRES → ENTRÉE LIBRE
GALA DROP, KIT W. HAWNAY TROOF,
FILIAMOTSA SOUFFLANT RHODES

VENDREDI 04 NOVEMBRE À 14H00
SAMEDI 05 NOVEMBRE À 13H00
LES TRINITAIRES → 3 €
ATELIER E-WASTE WORKSHOP 11.0,
DÉTOURNEMENT ET RECYCLAGE ÉLECTRONIQUE

SAMEDI 05 NOVEMBRE À 20H00
LES TRINITAIRES → 6 €
PERFORMANCE DE GIJS GIESKES
ET DE KARL KLOMP + TOKTEK

MARDI 08 NOVEMBRE À 20H00
LES TRINITAIRES → ENTRÉE LIBRE
SOIRÉE VIDÉO

JEUDI 10 NOVEMBRE À 21H00
COPRODUCTION CENTRE POMPIDOU-METZ ET MUSIQUES VOLANTES
CENTRE POMPIDOU-METZ → 10/15 €
SCOTT MATTHEW, PEDRO SOLER & GASPAR
CLAUS, AGATHE MAX, SELECTION WARP FILMS

VENDREDI 11 NOVEMBRE À 20H00
LES TRINITAIRES → 12/14 €
CHOKEBORE, ARTO LINDSAY, ANTILLES, OPERA
MORT, BASS DRUM OF DEATH, THE FEELING
OF LOVE, INSTALLATION CLIQUETIS DE VALENTIN
DURIF, MINI SILENT DISCO, BOMBAKLAK[VJ

SAMEDI 12 NOVEMBRE À 20H15
LES TRINITAIRES → 12/14 €
THE CHAP, THE JUAN MACLEAN, AFRIKAN BOY,
HOQUETS, UPROOT ANDY, MARIE MADELEINE,
INSTALLATION CLIQUETIS DE VALENTIN DURIF,
MINI SILENT DISCO, BOMBAKLAK[VJ

SAMEDI 12 NOVEMBRE À 16H00
DIMANCHE 13 NOVEMBRE À 16H00
CENTRE POMPIDOU-METZ → 5 €
POPUP PAR BELINDA ANNALORO
(SPECTACLE TOUS PUBLICS)

SOIRÉES SATELLITES

DU 3 AU 30 NOVEMBRE
STRASBOURG, STUTTGART,
PARIS, POITIERS, BORDEAUX, LUXEM-
BOURG, MONTPELLIER
THE PATRIOTIC SUNDAY, BRAIDS, CHEVEU, CIVIL
CIVIC, PNEU, ANIKA, GABLE, RUBIN STEINER
& IRA LEE...

INFORMATIONS

WWW.MUSIQUES-VOLANTES.ORG
+33(0)3 87 37 19 78
INFOS@MUSIQUES-VOLANTES.ORG
TARIF PASS 4 JOURS → 30 €
(VALABLE POUR LES CONCERTS DES 5, 10, 11
ET 12 NOVEMBRE)
LOCATIONS BILLETTERIE
RÉSEAU FNAC, CARREFOUR, GÉANT, INTERMARCHÉ
WWW.FNAC.COM · TEL : 0892 68 36 22 (0,34€/MIN)
WWW.DIGITICK.COM

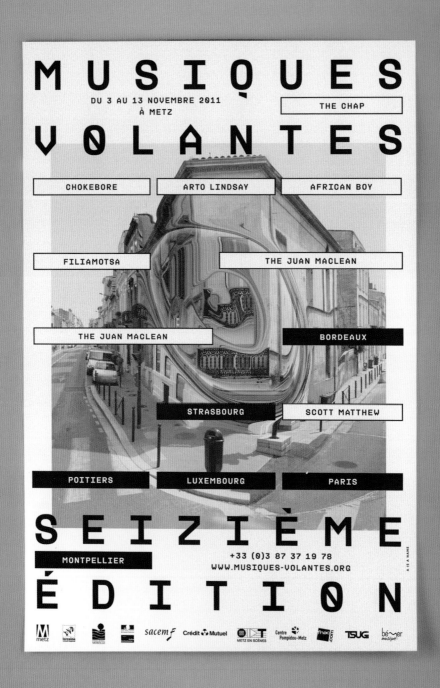

S for **Slam**

Slam is a personal work that explores the fusion of contemporary forms with aged images. The type design has taken references from Japanese signs, characters and vintage pictures of Judo players, with only the points of tension remained. A touch of red was added as a symbolic element of Japan.

Design : Sérgio Alves / Year : 2011

"COMMEDIA BUFFA"<<<<<<<

CO MM EDIA BU FFA

>>>>>>CRIAÇÃO COLECTIVA
>>>>>>>>>>>>>ENCENAÇÃO
>>>>>>>>LUCIANO AMARELO

PARTINDO DO "MISTERO<<<
BUFFO" DE DARIO FO,<<<<
ONDE SE FALA DOS<<<<<<<
JOGRAIS, DOS CONTADORES
E TRUÕES ITINERANTES<<<
QUE CONTRADIZIAM OS<<<<
EVANGELHOS OFICIAIS DA<
IGREJA, COM HISTÓRIAS<<
ORIGINÁRIAS DAS<<<<<<<<
TRADIÇÕES RELIGIOSAS<<<
E POPULARES, VAMOS<<<<<
EXPLORAR UM TEATRO<<<<<
ITINERANTE, PLENO<<<<<<
DE SÁTIRA, MÚSICA,<<<<<
MOVIMENTO E IMAGINAÇÃO.

>>>>>>>TOMANDO DEUS E O
>DIABO POR TESTEMUNHAS,
ENCENAREMOS O CAMPONÊS,
O VILÃO, A ALCOVITEIRA,
>>>>>>>>O ARISTOCRATA E
>>>>O PRELADO EM TEXTOS
>>>>DE TEMPOS PASSADOS,
>>SEMPRE COM UM SORRISO
>>>NOS LÁBIOS E O BUFÃO
>>>>COMO NOSSO MESTRE
>>>>>>>>DE CERIMÓNIAS.

SALA ESTÚDIO LATINO<<<
(TEATRO SÁ DA BANDEIRA)<<
11 A 15 DE DEZEMBRO<<<<
22:00<<<<<<<<<<<<<<<<<<

ESTRUTURA FINANCIADA POR:
WWW.TERRANABOCA.COM

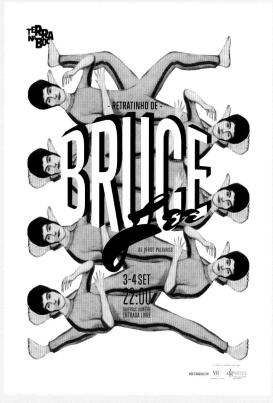

T for
Terra na Boca
Poster Series

Terra na Boca is a cultural organisation focused on theatrical art. Consistent with the elements of collage art, manipulated types and a touch of contemporary arts and crafts, the posters individually introduce a programme or event with a distinctive look.

Design : Sérgio Alves / Client : Terra na Boca / Year : 2010

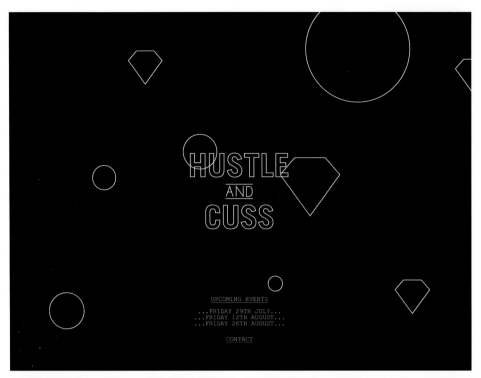

H for **Hustle and Cuss**

Hustle and Cuss is an underground night club in Birmingham. The simplistic yet classic graphic identity has been commissioned to reflect their gothic overtones.

Design : Family / Photography : Mezzetty / Client : Hustle & Cuss / Year : 2011

HUSH AND CUSS

	JULY		AUGUST		AUGUST
29TH	ROOM 1 CHRIS WOODS	12TH	ROOM 1 CHRIS WOODS	26TH	ROOM 1 CHRIS WOODS
	ROOM 2 JOHAN WESK		ROOM 2 MICHAEL T		ROOM 2 SUZIE MASON

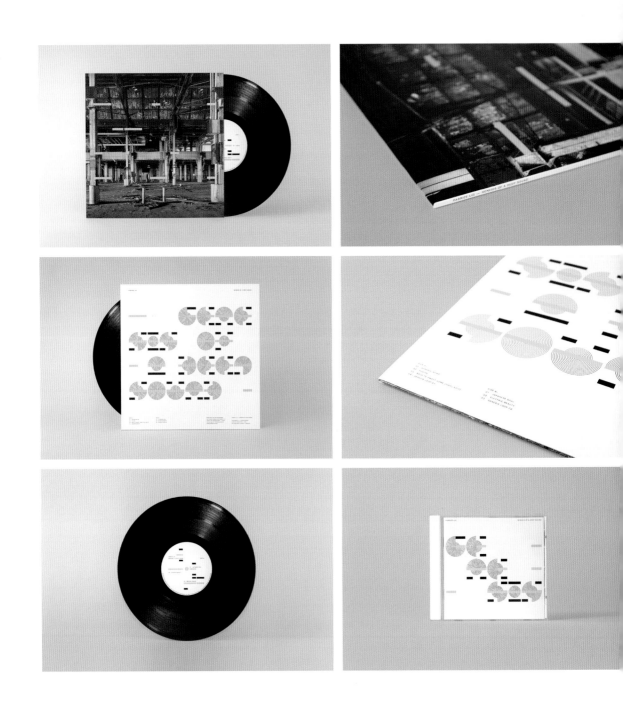

F for **Fabrice Lig**

Packaging for techno music producer Fabrice Lig's LP
record, *Genesis of a Deep Sound*. The abstracted typographic
system has been developed to resonate with their music that
pays homage to a mix of techno heros.

Design : Sawdust / Creative Production : Edit / Photography : Andrew
Moore / Client : Fine Art Recordings / Year : 2010

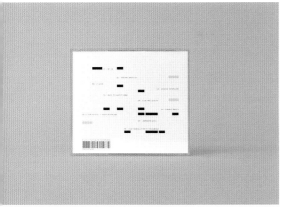

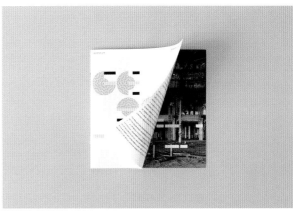

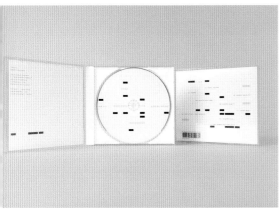

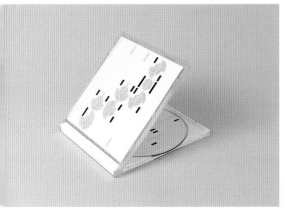

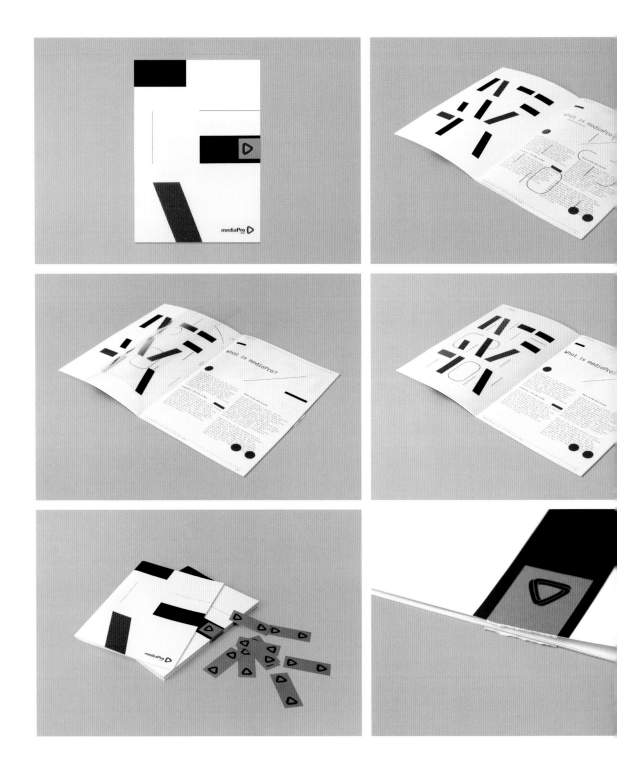

M for **mediaPro**

Printed material for mediaPro, a London-based event focused on the
future of integrated marketing and communications. Two sets of lines and
shapes were printed on separate pages to express the word 'integration'
when the pages overlay.

Design : Sawdust / Client : Yum Yum / CloserStill / Year : 2010

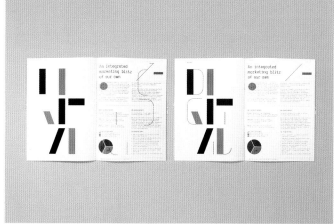

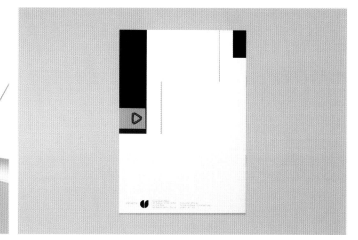

MARKETING MUSIC   LABEL NIGHT

FRIDAY 25TH NOV · 2011   AT EAST VILLAGE

EAST VILLAGE
89 GREAT EASTERN
STREET
EC2A 3HX
LONDON

WITH
EWAN PEARSON
(KOMPAKT/SOMA)
[3HRS SET]
TIM PARIS
(MARKETING MUSIC)

10PM-3.30AM
6£ BEFORE 11PM
8£ AFTER
(5£ PREPAID)
ADVANCE TICKETS
WWW.RESIDENTADVISOR.NET
& WWW.TICKETWEB.CO.UK

M for
Marketing Music

Tim Paris has founded his music label at London. He called it
Marketing Music because of the particular relation between
music creation and the music market. A typographic system
was specially made to bespeak the idea in his identity and print
communication.

Design : A is a name / Client : Tim Paris / Marketing Music / Year : 2009-11

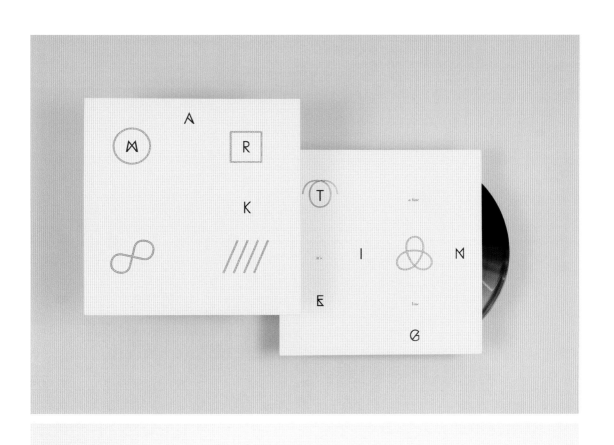

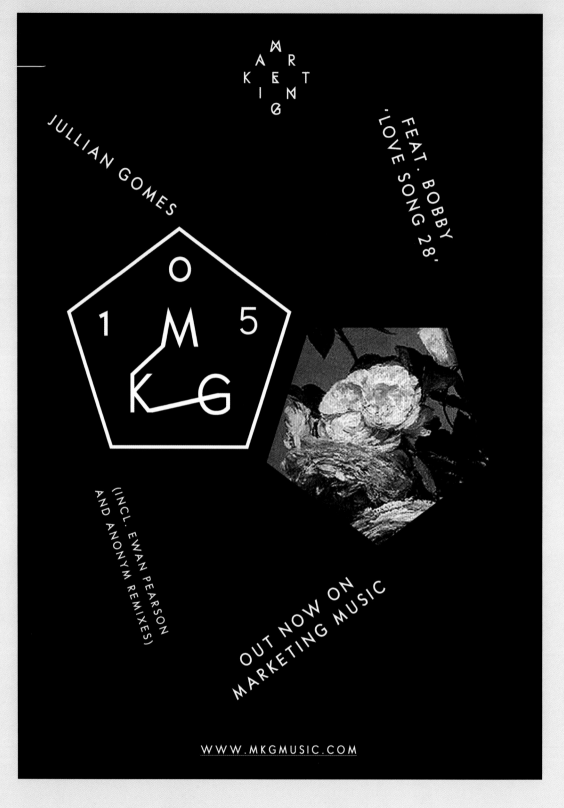

BRAWNY GODS
JUST FLOCKED UP
TO QUIZ
AND VEX HIM.

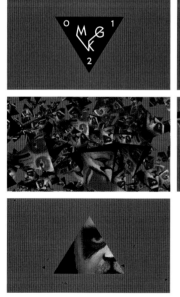

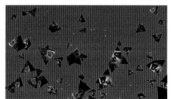

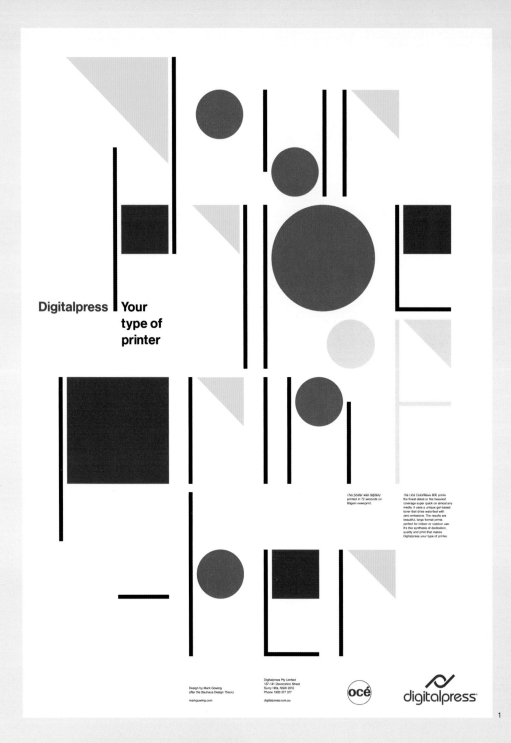

L for **Letters in Shape**

Posters to promote digital printer, Digitalpress, using primary colours to harness their printing techniques; and 2010 Icograda Design Week in Brisbane. Geometric forms were respectively references of Bauhaus aesthetics and Australian natural landscape.

Design : Mark Gowing Design

1 Your Type of Printer /
Digitalpress / 2010
2 Optimism Australia Conference /
Icograda / 2010

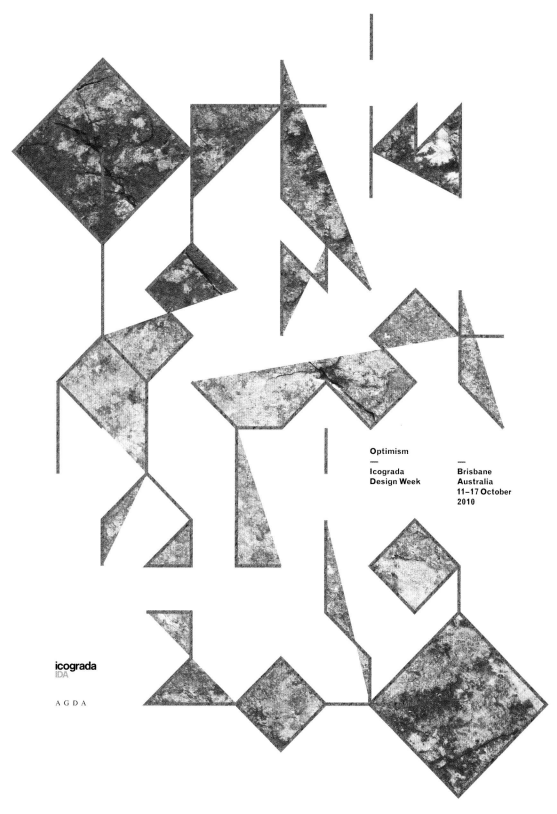

Optimism
—
Icograda
Design Week

—
Brisbane
Australia
11–17 October
2010

icograda
IDA

A G D A

D for **Dreams Come True**

Ribbon lettering purely shaped with silken threads and photographed for
the tour book to be sold at Japanese band, DREAMS COME TRUE's
concert, WONDERLAND 2011.

Design : NAM / Client : Sony Music Communications / Year : 2011

P for
Photography

A moment of calm reflection to celebrate the enormous anticipation and frantic yet methodical approach to set up a photo shoot and also the aftermath. Cover art for *Creative Review*'s annual photography issue.

Design : Jiggery Pokery / Photography : Annie Collinge / Client : Creative Review / Year : 2010

G for **Ghent Creative City**

The four big letters spelling GENT (Ghent) portray Ghent's way of life on the outskirts and inside the city in scale models. The project was produced for an initiative of the city council of Ghent where local creative forces gather to shape the city's future in forms of art.

Design : Soon / Client : City of Ghent / Year : 2010

T for
Type & Environment

A photographic project showing that typography can take a variety of forms and textures and integrate into landscapes of any kind. The compositions are always different, but the concept remains the same.

Design : Pierre Delort / Photography : Samuel Guigues / Year : 2010

A for **A Vanishing Point**

"There is no mirage without a vanishing point" is an extract from Vladimir Nabokov's *Transparent Things* (1972). The idea is rendered with an illusion of forward movements realised in layers of handpainted acetate sheets, backlit by lightbox.

Design : Alida Rosie Sayer / Photography : Philip Sayer, Alida Rosie Sayer / Year : 2011

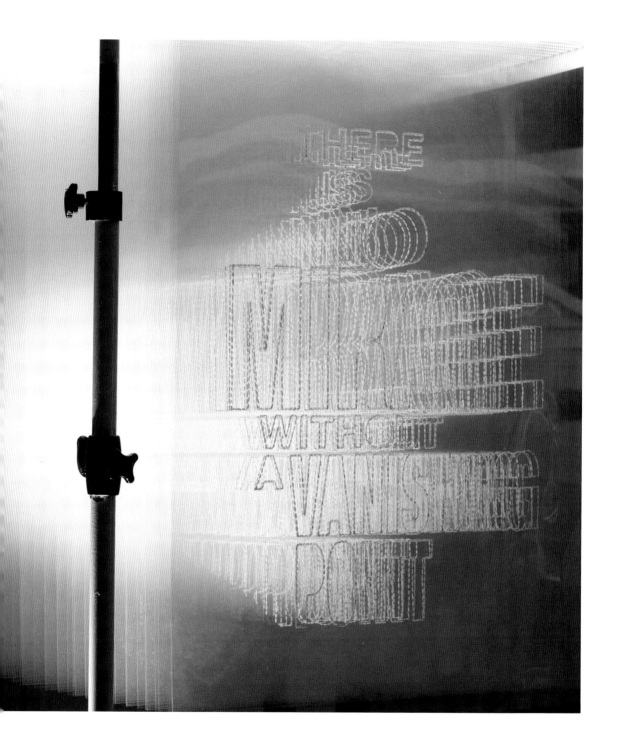

THERE
IS
NO
MIRAGE
WITHOUT
A VANISHING
POINT

W for **What I Saw**

Dimensionally handcrafted out of one stack of identically printed double-sided paper, the four sculptural pieces explore the idea of transcendence in space and depth, inspired by *The Mirror* (1983) by Haruki Murakami.

Design : Alida Rosie Sayer / Photography : Philip Sayer / Year : 2011

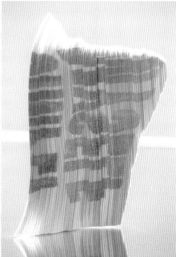

A for **All Moments**

A project that explores time and memory visualisation with concepts and quotes drawn from *Slaughterhouse Five* (1969) by Kurt Vonnegut. The entire collection was printed and cut by hand.

Design : Alida Rosie Sayer / Year : 2009

E for **Eternity**

A time-based installation made from 30 analogue clocks, each set to indicate a different "time" and spell the word "Eternity" once every 12 hours. As soon as the hands begin to move, the word would immediately fall apart into a jumble of black lines.

Design : Alicia Eggert and Mike Fleming / Year : 2010

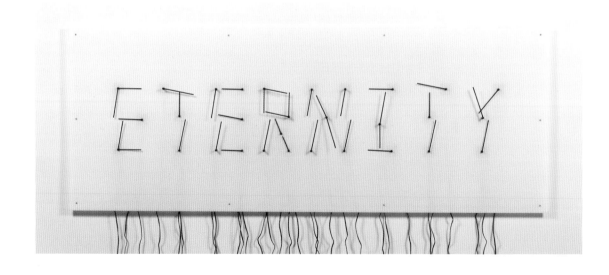

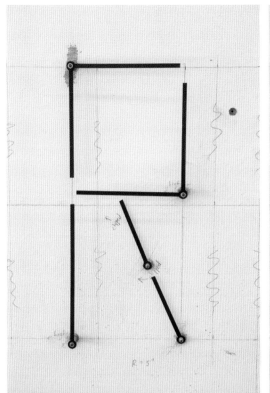

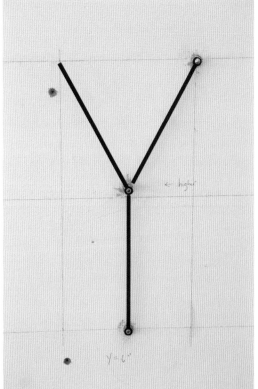

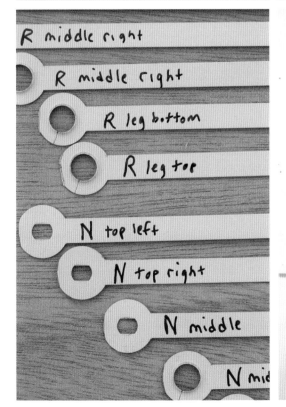

R middle right

R middle right

R leg bottom

R leg top

N top left

N top right

N middle

N mid

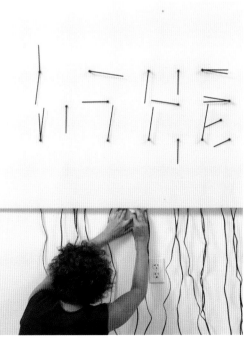

C for **CNJPUS TEXT**

CNJPUS TEXT represents the segment of Japanese who simply adopts foreign influences in their immediate environment. The text is a compound of Chinese characters and English's spacing arrangements. The project's title alludes to its elements with the countries' top-level domain codes.

Design : Ryo Shimizu / Year : 2009-

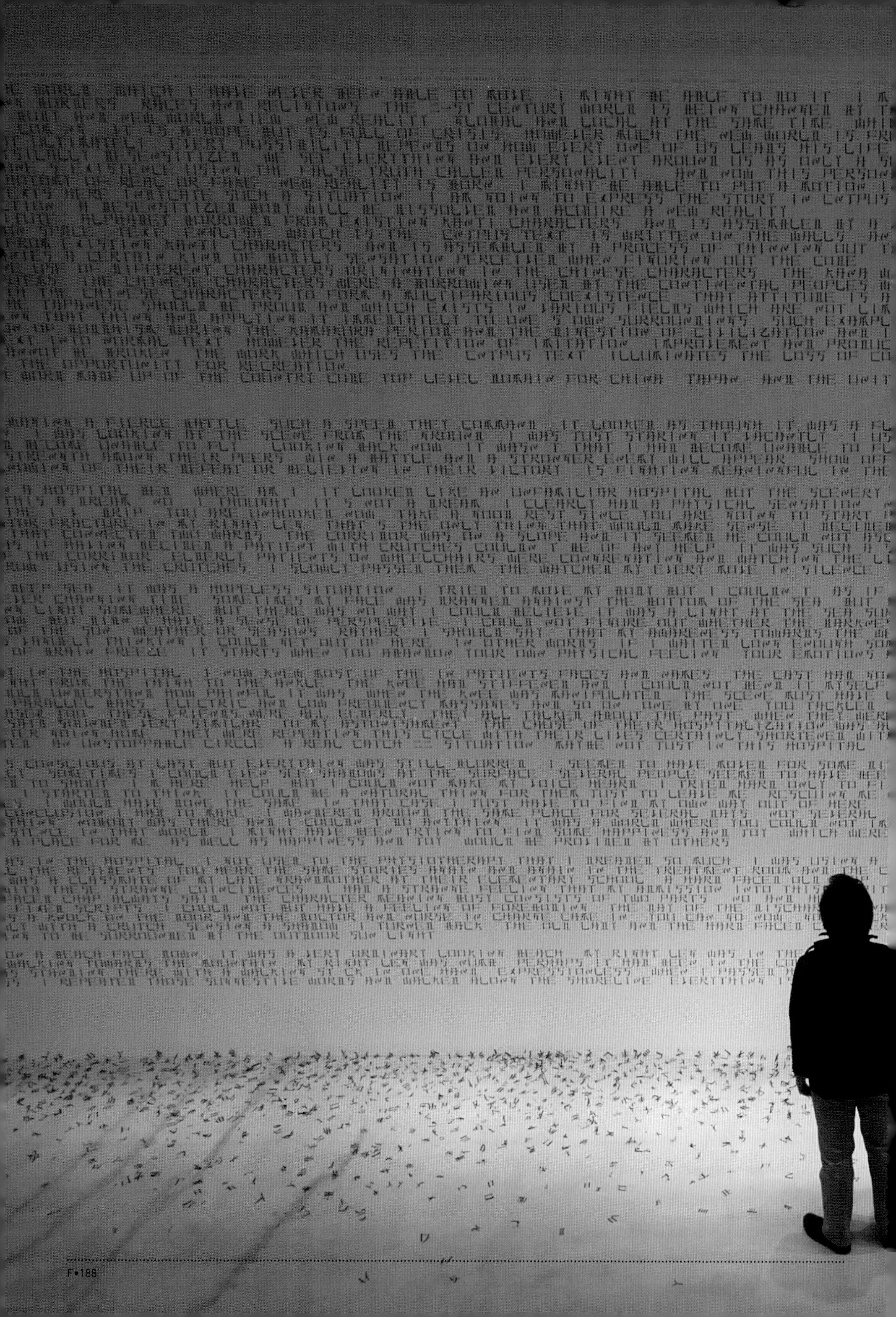

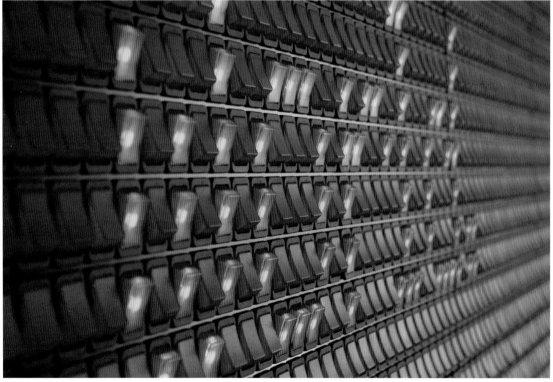

H for **Hello World.**

An installation art piece that plays on the binary nature of the on/off switches to phrase the message "Hello World" just as how one of the world's earliest computer programmes greeted. The work measures 185 centimetres by 265 centimetres.

Design : Valentin Ruhry / Year : 2011

F for **Forgive Me!!**

Composed of fluorescent tubes, spaced out over a wood panel to spell "FORGIVE ME!!", the light installation asked its viewers to resolve the message which pleads for forgiveness.

Design : Valentin Ruhry / Year : 2007

A for
Alphabet Series

Using the creative tool of perspectives, *Alphabetical Series* is
a unique photographic collection dedicated to alphabets and
Helvetica. The medium of construction was distinct, ranging from
painted objects carefully arranged against monotone backgrounds
to light projection on natural landscape.

Design : Dan Tobin Smith Studio / Year : 2007-

Set Design : Nicola Yeoman

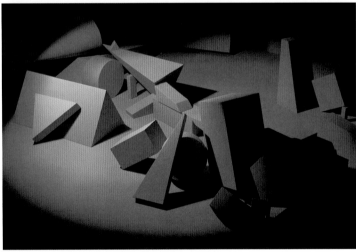

Special Effects, Settings : Asylum SFX

it's a
point of
view

A for
Anamorphic
Typography

Viewers are invited to physically immerse in types within the
same space they stand in which the installations adorn. The
phrases also express a comment on the conventional way to
present graphic art.

Design : Joseph Egan, Hunter Thomson / Photography : Alex Madjitey
(Chelsea College of Art & Design Photography Department) / Year : 2010

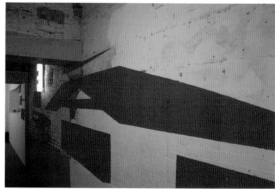

IT'S MORE THAN JUST PRINT

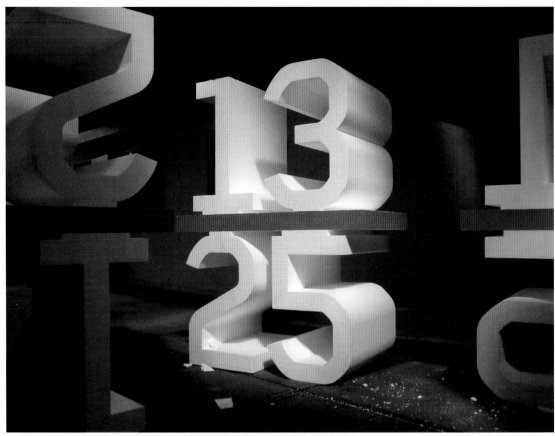

U for
Utrecht Uitfeest
Leidsche Rijn

Visual identity and typographic wayfinding system routing along 25 works of art artworks at Utrecht Uitfeest Leidsche Rijn. The artificial blocks were laser-crafted out of sustainable polystyrene to draw attention and stand out against the wide and open space.

Design : Autobahn / Client : City of Utrecht / Year : 2008

L for **LIGHT LOOM**

Installation to celebrate the 50th anniversary of Canon Neoreal Wonder Milano Salone. The notion was to build a new relationship with light, so by tracing the radiating light beams with countless strings, the light is given substance in space.

Exhibition Space Design : Torafu Architects / Production : TRUNK / Supervision : ZITOMORI / Visual Design : WOW / Graphic Design : TAKAIYAMA inc. / Photography : Daici Ano, Daisuke Ohki, Daisuke Shimokawa / Exhibition Site : Superstudio Più ART POINT / Client : Canon / Year : 2011

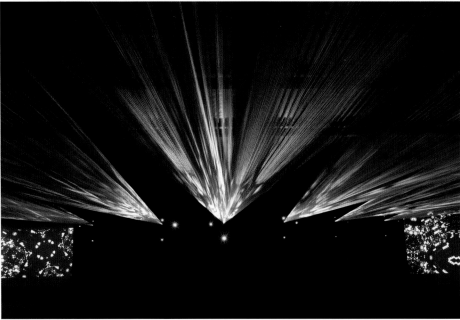

TYPO
HOLIC
A TO Z

Type design is a commitment to create an alphabetical family. It challenges designers to create and publish the face of no less than 26 letters at a time, each distinct in character, affiliated by affinity yet versatile in use. Distinctively expressive and appealing to our eyes, the chapter exhibits 27 meticulously composed typefaces underlaid by strong creative notions and foundations.

FOREWORD BY SERGIO DEL PUERTO SERIAL CUT™

Type is communication and should be a testimony of our days. I have been always in love with type. Since I was a child, I always had some kind of sensibilty about type. I saw clearly what types should be used in the layout of the School Newspaper while my classmates don't, so eventually I took care of this type part. I also loved the toys packaging and kept them for their bright type colours as a reference.

Besides my studio's attempt to create contemporary — I don't like the word "modern" — images, I think the best projects are the ones containing classic types, which persist in time, and the combination with more modern elements gets a timeless result. For me is the only way to keep my images, my artworks actual.

I usually search for new types and keep previews in a folder as a "wish list" and then I buy them very often. The WOW factor is crucial. I don't need a really complicated type, like the broken or very curly ones, to get surprised but first and foremost they have to be readable, memorable and original, simple with a "twist". I also look for font families as well as the display ones that migh fit our compositions with 3D elements. But I have to say that nowadays not many new types surprised me, I see repetitions all the time, but of course there are some new classics, like Gotham, Neutra, Graphic, Amplitude or Freight.

I have to mention one of my type heroes, Herb Lubalin, the man who gave me total inspiration in type. Through his type treatments,

I really learn a way to make something clean, contemporary but also with a retro feel. Ideas never come at once. We usually look at some old issues of *U&LC* and always find something that could be done nowadays. That's good design. Timeless.

We have been working on type treatments since we started the studio, and in the last few years we have been "kind of brave" while we experiment with type. For us it's a bit dated using just a simple typical extruded type, which many people make these days. So now the big aim is to bring the audience something more advanced, like how we explored the medium of type-making to elevate the capacity of words with roller coaster rails, jelly, skin, ham or clay. All of them can be seen in this book. So the idea is that type composition finally works like itself as a stunning image and communication itself.

FOREWORD BY JOSEPH EGAN

Typography in its simplest form is the visualisation of language.

Language is the basis of human communication.

The ability to communicate goes hand in hand with advances in technology.

As a designer you should always be interested in new technology, understanding it and exploring its potential to create work. Technology however, is just a tool, one that can be a large destroyer of feeling and truth within typography and graphic design in general. Learning about past technologies like letterpress and calligraphy will help you understand where to take your ideas and processes in the future, more so than being the best at Photoshop.

Live for ideas, they are the backbone of your work and are what make it last. Constantly read books, explore ideas and expand your vocabulary. The more you talk, read and write about type and design then the more confident you will become in your work and the better your work will be overall.

As an experimental typographer you should understand the absolute basics of typography and the art of making and placing marks on a physical surface. Learning the rules now will help make you a better designer and to know when to disregard

them completely. Design is a craft and by using your hands to create work it will have a certain degree of irregularity for which no apology is needed and a feeling of warmth that does not exist inside the digital realm.

A piece of type that you can touch, walk round and look through will always be more interesting than the same thing on a screen, if only because it is not what we (as readers) are used to. Take typography to another level and make people question their conventional relationship with it outside the 2D plain. Physical type should be fun and engaging to both the eye and the mind, always challenging and never misspelt. Bigger is always better, and remember...

The medium is the message.

Alphabet

Stuart Whitton

Alphabet is entirely cast out of fashion items. Accurate and explicitly traced, each of these characters is the pencil sketch of 26 different fashion articles, deliberately stylised to create the specific shapes of the 26 alphabets. The curation of items and way they were set lend the type a free and easy touch.

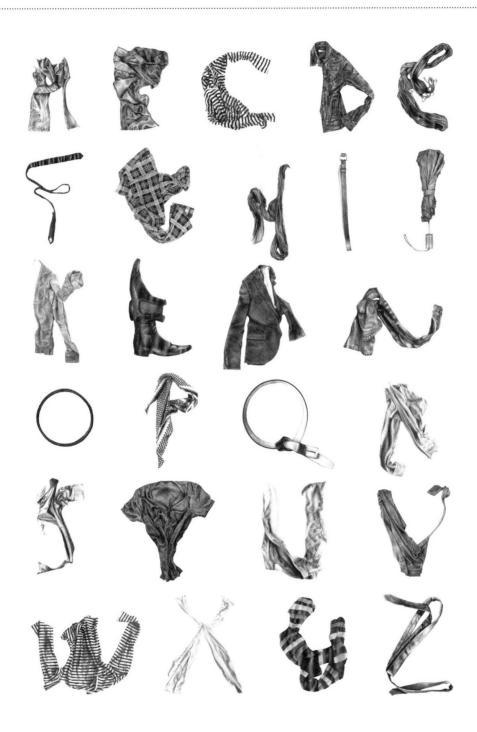

Elastic

Jenny Kyvik Hutchens

Elastic is the designer's school project at Westerdals with its composition entirely relied on the wise distribution of pins and rubberbands. The original results and model has lasted for two months before the bands started to snap.

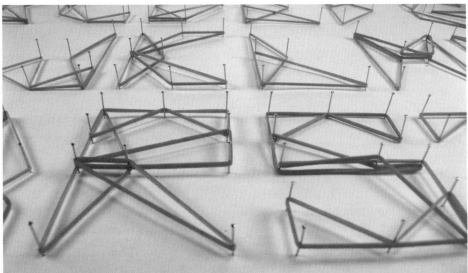

Take a Seat and Say Something

Amandine Alessandra

The *Take a Seat and Say Something* series has used a chair as a matrix to compose 26 alphabets. Partially covered up in cloth and sketch pads, these chairs constitute a challenge to read individually but become comprehensible once they are put together as words.

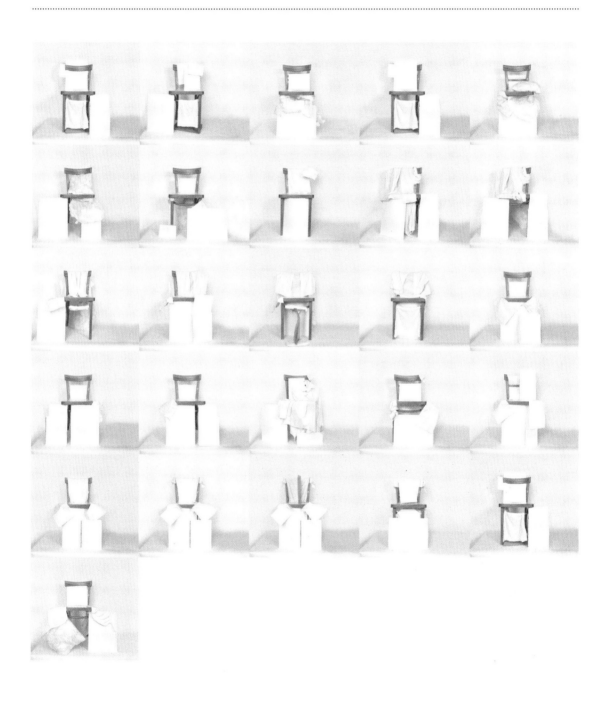

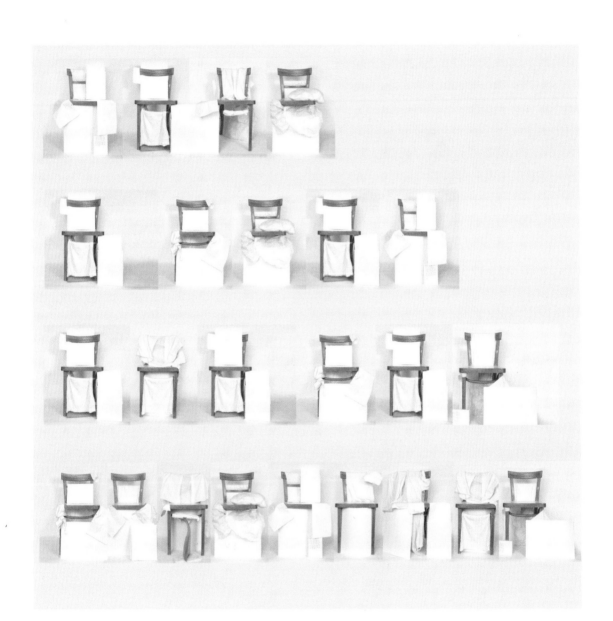

Animal Fonts

KOTENHITS, Daisy Balloon

With heat taken as the idea of global warming and jinx on balloons, *Animal Fonts* forms a statement about environmental issues, with animals shaped into the first letter of their names to compose messages in a phone app. The app also features multiple tunes, collected in a CD, to celebrate the preciousness of the nature.

Sound Leo Sato / **System Management** 8UNITE / **CD Packaging Paper** Heiwa Paper Co., Ltd.

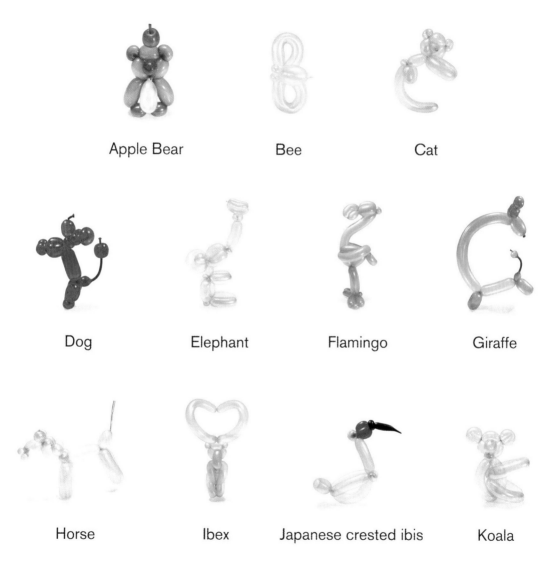

Apple Bear   Bee   Cat

Dog   Elephant   Flamingo   Giraffe

Horse   Ibex   Japanese crested ibis   Koala

Lion

Mouse

Nessie

Orangutan

Penguin

Qtaro

Roadrunner

Snake

Tree

Unicorn

Vulture

Weasel

Xenopus

Yak

Zebra

"Pray for Japan"

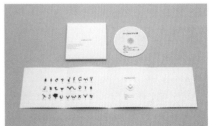

Train Set Typography

Burcau Bruncau (Ludvig Bruneau Rossow)

The defined structure of railway networks has established this typeface's unique forms, such as the 'E' and 'Z', that would cause one to wonder if they could possibly exist in real life. The set is an experimental project based on an old train set which Ludvig Bruneau Rossow found in his grandmother's basement.

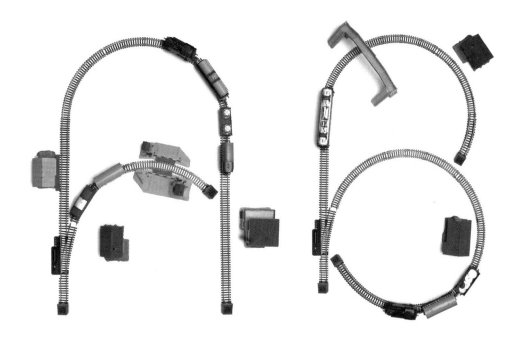

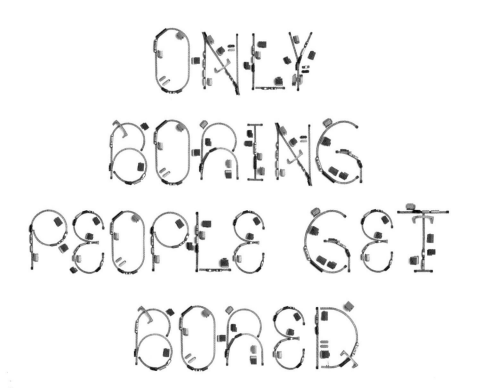

ONLY BORING PEOPLE GET BORED

Heterosis — A Kinetic Typeface

Brian Banton

Heterosis has been initiated with a vision to produce letters with its volume built out of lines. These lines are drawn from one panel to another, weaving into multidimensional alphabets as planes hanging in space. The models were constructed with transparent elastic bands and acrylic boards, with advice from David Scadding, Jan Hadlaw and Paul Sych.

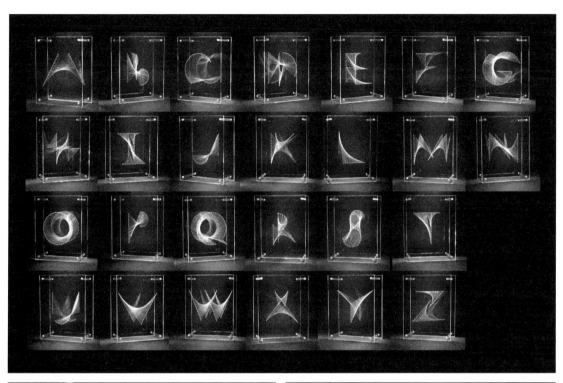

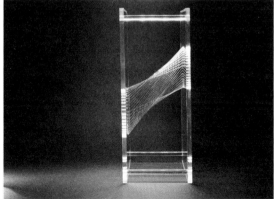

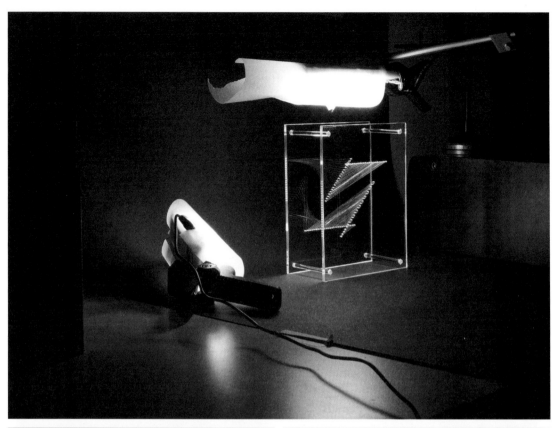

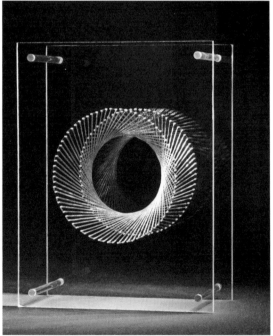

Type Fluid

Skyrill.com

Type Fluid is the experimental combination of letterforms and liquids which take exquisite forms as they drip, flow and splash. The concept was to capture the interesting moments and energy of flying liquids before they totally lost their recognisable alphabetical forms.

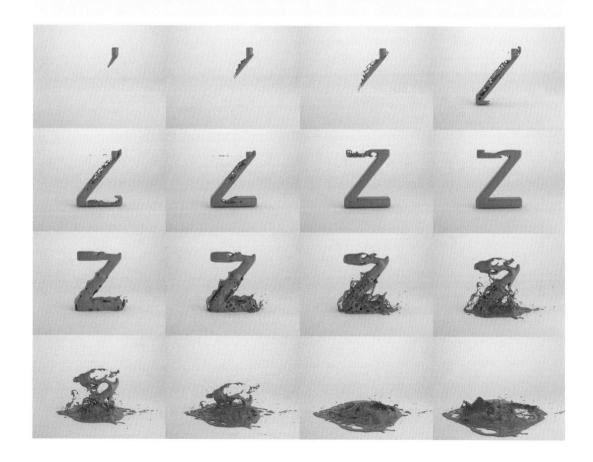

Weave Type II

Zim&Zou

The second edition of *Weave* type continues to be a piece of handwork based on thread but embroidered on paper. Composed of numerous sets of radial lines in three colours, each character conveys a delicate. fragmented pattern within an invisible frame. The process has approximately taken up six hours and 500 metres of thread to complete.

Living Typography

Nishant Jethi

The declining conditions of natural habitats for sparrows and thus their numbers in busy cities have led to the building of *Living Typography*, with bird houses adopting typographic forms to connect its notions with man. The houses are currently installed in Mumbai where the least sparrows can be found in India.

Special Credits Mudra Communications, Water Design Studio

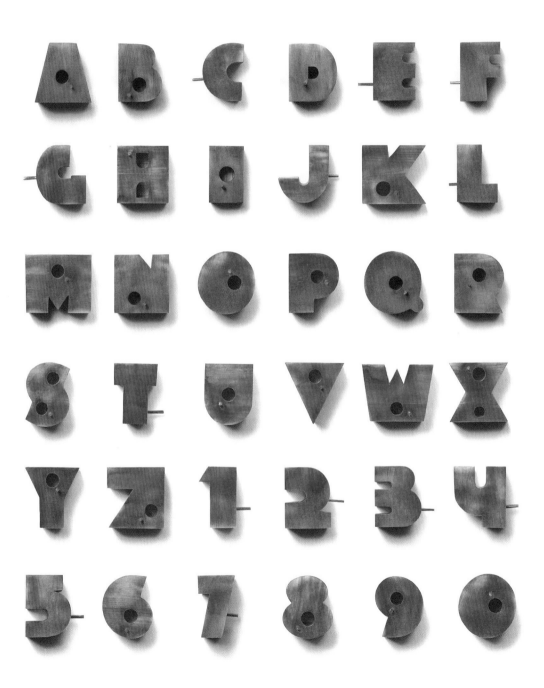

The Ultimate Alphabet

Jerome Corgier

The Ultimate Alphabet is Jerome Corgier's personal experiment with creating an animation only with type. Varied in forms but united by their medium, these paper letters are designed to speak and express on their own. The final alphabets are a display of characters distinguished by colours and patterns, and realised based on typeface, Whitney.

Dirt Type

Form Follows Freedom

Dirt Type contains no dirt at all. The alphabets and punctuations series made out of coloured and snipped brooms was designed as one of the multiple green expressions at exhbition "Garden at Home" by AT CASA in Fuorisalone 2011.
Punctuations like comma are featured in different typefaces, such as Comic sans and Helvetica Neue Heavy.

Booksetting

Amandine Alessandra

Booksetting reinterprets Thomas Fuller's statement "A book that is shut is but a block" and argues that "shut books" are more than "blocks" since they speak. The making is said to be reminiscent of typesetting, with books in colours blocked with the white ones. The shelves here were taken as the common typographic grid.

Troberg

HelloMe

Troberg is an electropop band from Munich whose music is a multifarious mix of dark synthesizer, bossanova drums, accordion, strings, children's keyboard and a strong female vocal. The visual system for the band's namesake album is the expressive, organic form of their sound and poetic lyrics, painted by hand.

Client Ground, Troberg

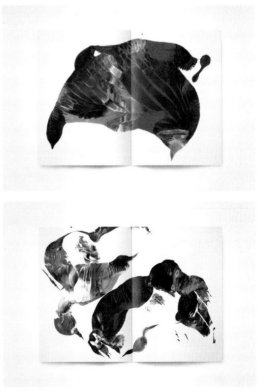

Bedsheet Typography

Bravo Company

While type manics dream of typography in their sleep, Bravo's designers climbed out of bed and made types out of their own bed sheets. The collection has a combination of mixed lettercases, which pleasantly surprise the makers with their brush-like strokes.

Photography Lumina Studio

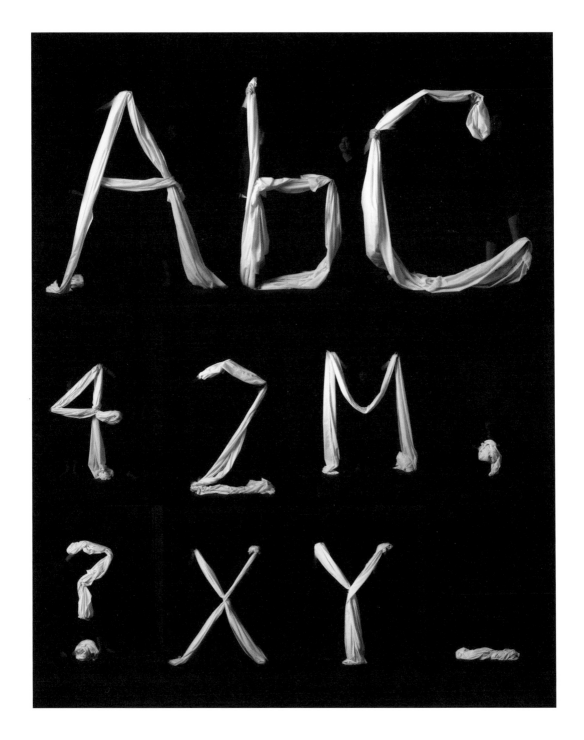

MEKKANIKA

Riccardo Sabatini

Inspired by old mechanics technical drawings, *MEKKANIKA* is the hybrid of modern and anachronistic machinery in the letter shapes of the DIN Alternate Black. The mechanical look was achieved through its details and complexity one could find in machinery.

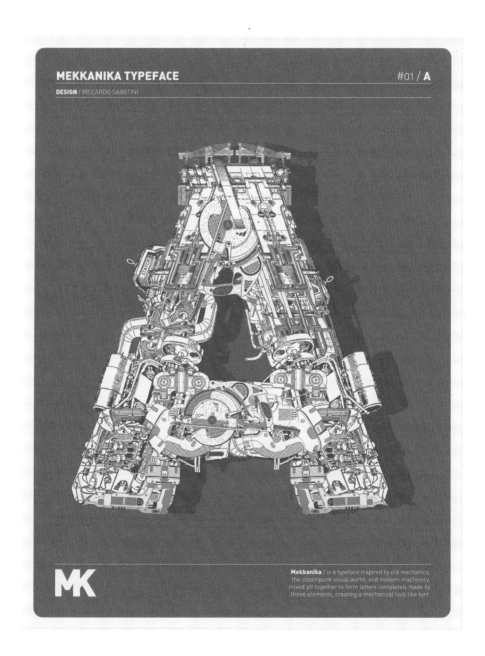

MEKKANIKA TYPEFACE #01 / **A**
DESIGN / RICCARDO SABATINI

MK

Mekkanika / is a typeface inspired by old mechanics, the steampunk visual world, and modern machinery, mixed all together to form letters completely made by these elements, creating a mechanical look like font.

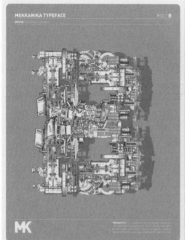

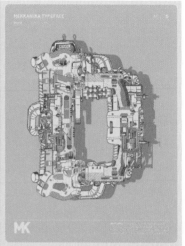

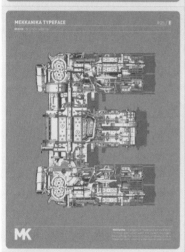

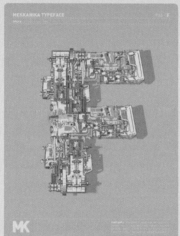

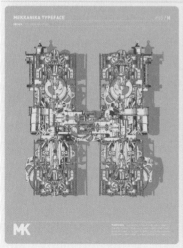

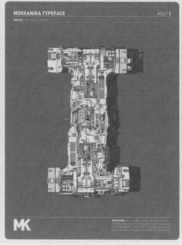

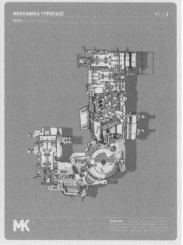

MEKKANIKA

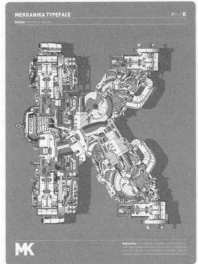

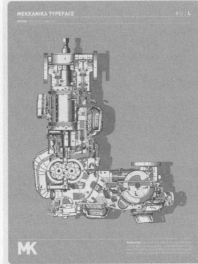

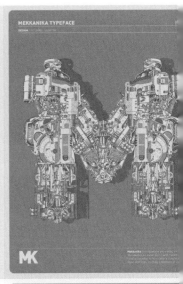

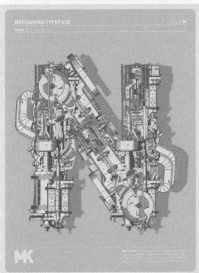

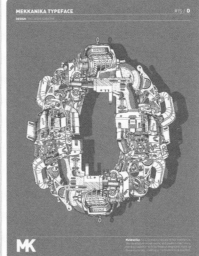

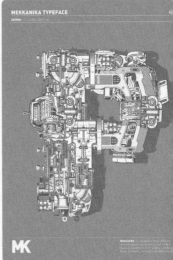

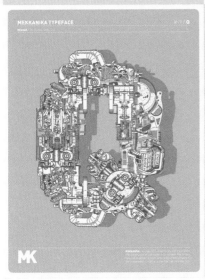

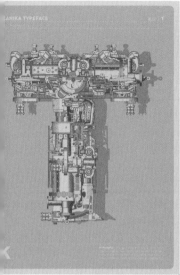

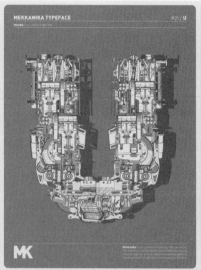

MK

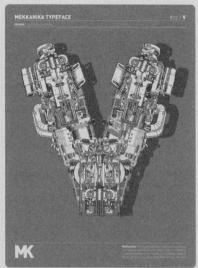

MK

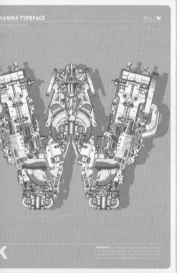

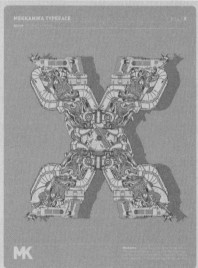

MK

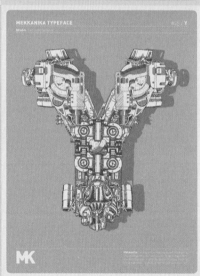

MK

K

Playful

Plenty

Suggested by its name, *Playful* is a playful and experimental composition of letters, numbers and punctuations characterised by its exaggerated weight and geometric components. Solid and robust, the typeface challenges readers' idea of standard letters in its flat and dimensional forms.

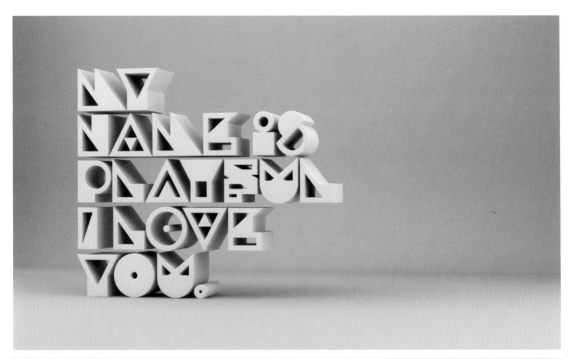

Coral

Txaber Mentxaka

Like a cluster of red blood cells clinging together, each of these characters' surface renders a layer of coral structure which gives the typeface its name. The typeface has two digital variants, flat and as three-dimensional figures as featured.

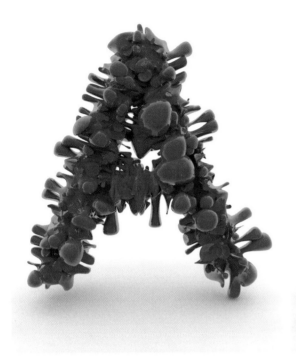

Globe

Txaber Mentxaka

Constructed like inflated balloons with a sealed edge suspended in the air, the *Globe* family attributes liveliness and flexibility to words as users tilt or shift the letters like they are really spinning in the air. The mutable shadows help to solidify the effect.

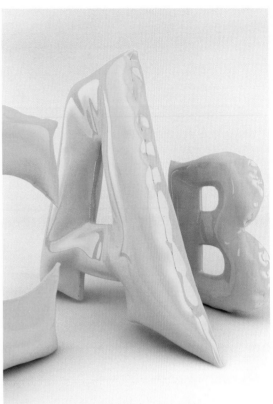

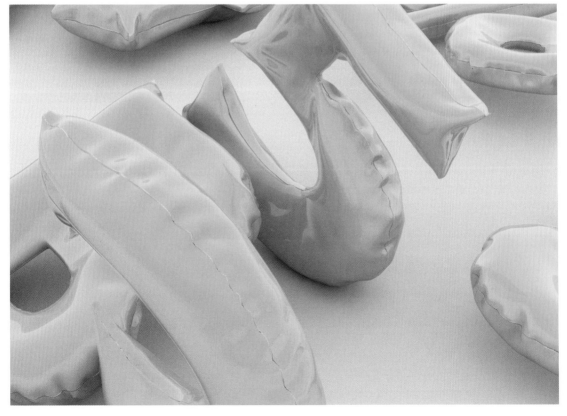

Wood

Txaber Mentxaka

Structured with an irregular surface, these block types offer variations in its form and volume if viewed from a different perspective. The strong sculptural quality of wood finish adds a sense of tactility to the digitally rendered block letter set.

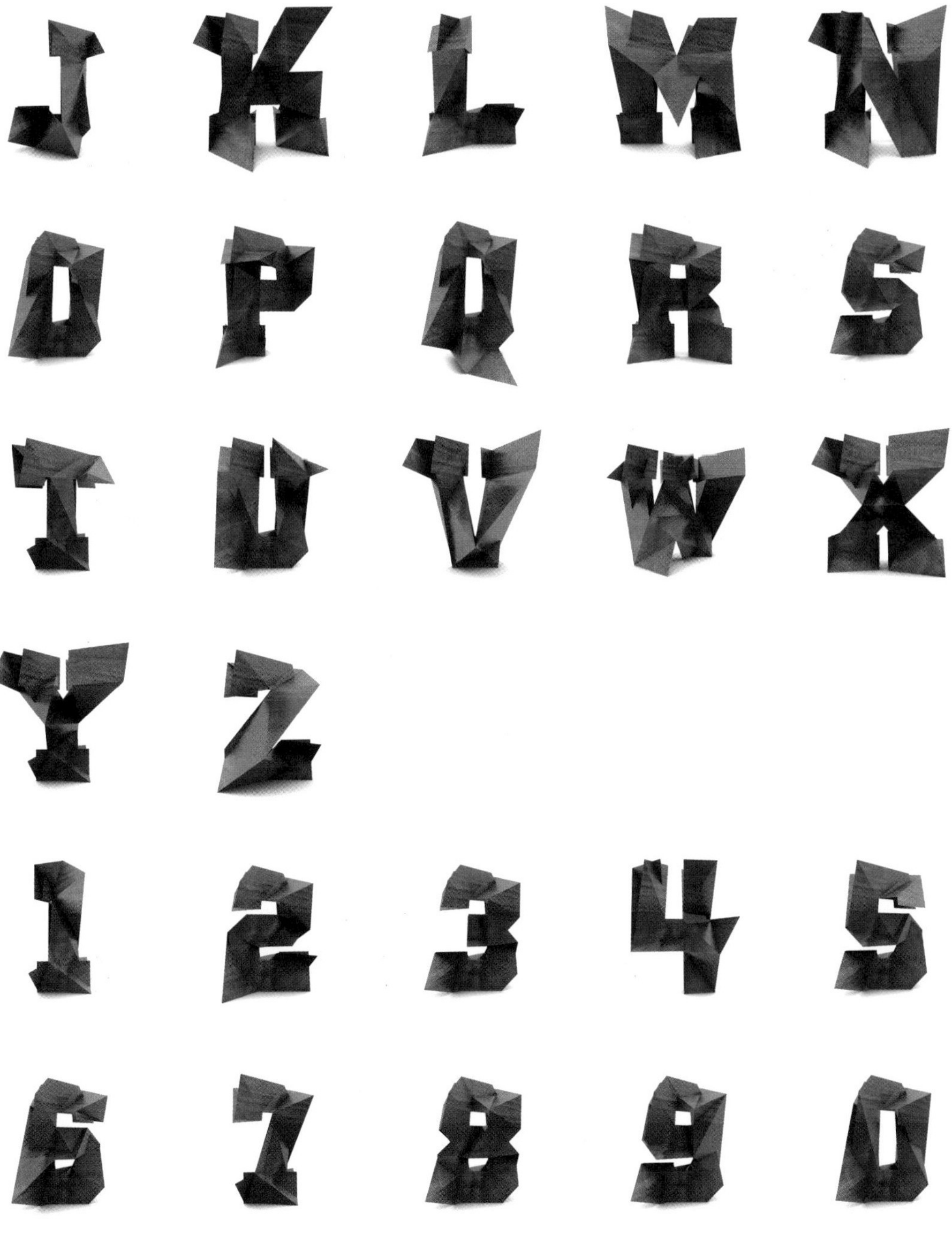
J K L M N
O P Q R S
T U V W X
Y Z
1 2 3 4 5
6 7 8 9 0

Supersic 58

Txaber Mentxaka

Its superimposed sequin-like layers are integral to this typeface. Where gradations accentuate the sense of depth in each alphabet, the alphabets offer an illusion of space as the colours vary according to its position in application. The name of the type is Txaber Mentxaka's tribute to the late Italian motobike racer, Marco Simoncelli.

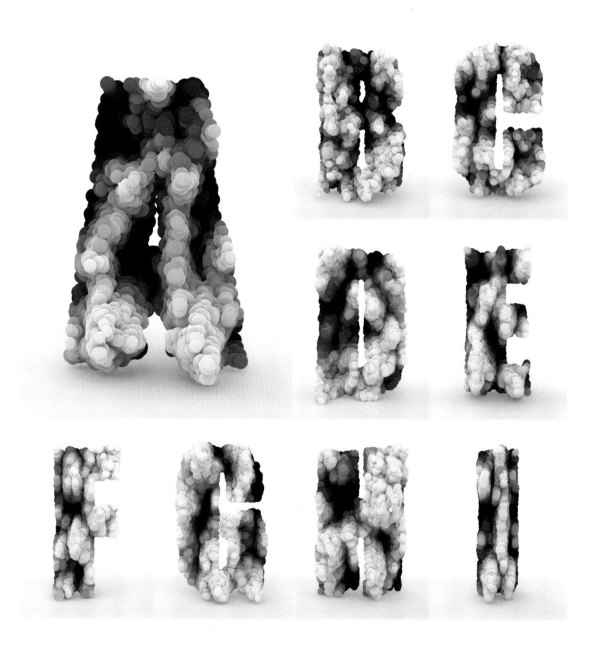

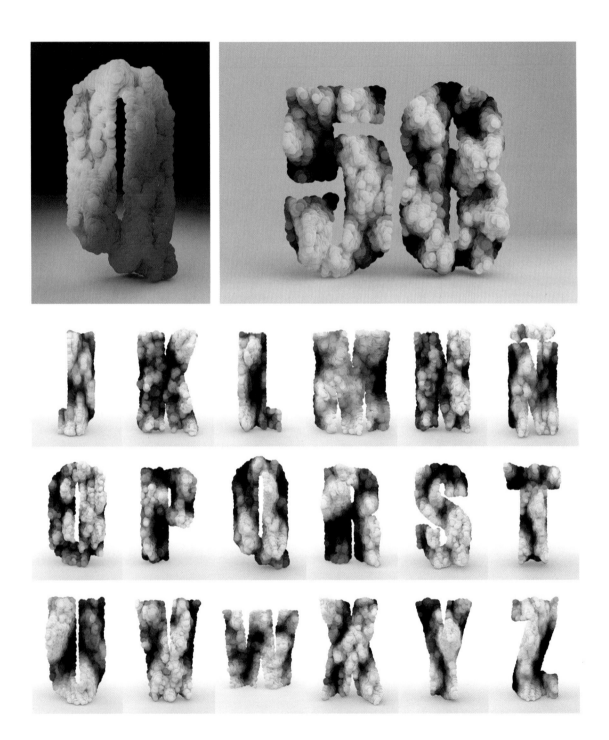

Roke1984

Joan Ramon Pastor

Roke1984 is a display font based on the measurement of shapes, such as angles and their numeral values, to celebrate geometric properties indicated by mathematic marks. The typeface conveys technicality and science and is devised for a highly mathematical look.

Poster Design Pau Molas

QUANTUM
DISCOTHEQUE
FULL MOON
WATER CLOSED
RIGHT
MAGENTA 123

WE LIKE
TO CREATE
BIZARRE
FORM
STRUCTURES
TO PRODUCE
GREAT FONTS

GEEKPOWER
MATHEMATICS III
COOL STYLE
1984 ASTRO
9 PHYSICS
GALILEO
UNIVERSITY

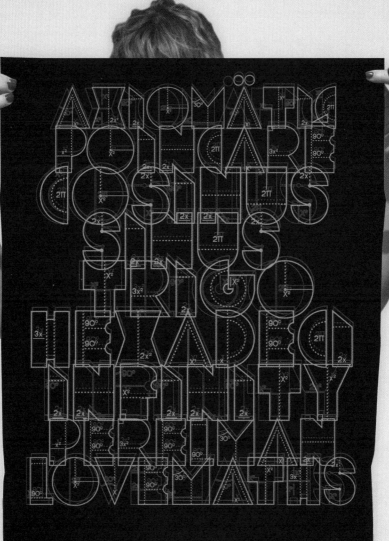

Dance With Me

Amandine Alessandra

Dance With Me is a choreographic piece captured with long-exposure photography which would otherwise be invisible to the naked eye. The 26 alphabets are composed of a designed sequence of arm movements captured in special lighting conditions to highlight the dancers' arms.

Kids Alphabet

NAM

Made possible by Better Light scanning backs' unstable qualities, alphabets in this series are playfully interpreted as children explored their body movements and interacted with their surroundings. Each stroke traces movements contrasting its static background, resulting in delightful distortions and amusing artistic effects.

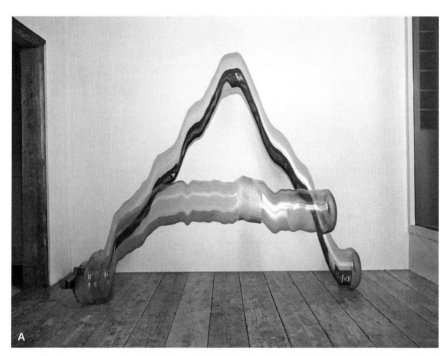

A

B

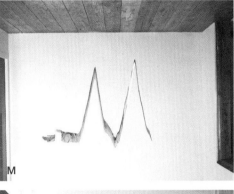

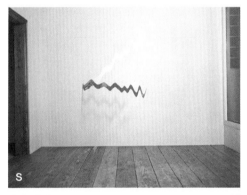

Asialphabet

Yoriko Youda

While 'A' is for 'Akita', 'B' for 'Bonsai', *Asialphabet* gives alphabets an oriental twist. Letters from the set are extracted as the staples of Japanese culture, such as a contorted Geisha or a twisted bonsai tree. The result is a classic set of uber-imaginative art that Yoriko Youda can be proud of.

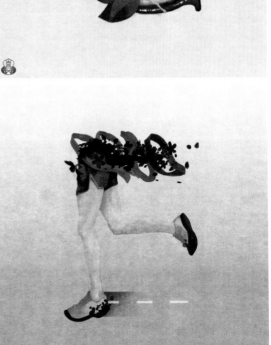

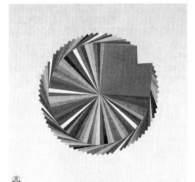

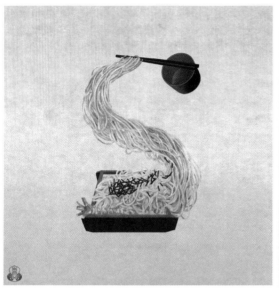

What Are You Afraid Of?

Senongo Akpem

Suggested in its name, each letter of the font is made up of a different nightmare inducer based on all of the designer's own greatest fears. His personal favourite letter is said to be the letter 'B'. The imagery displays a tapeworm in a beautiful, yet oddly disturbing light.

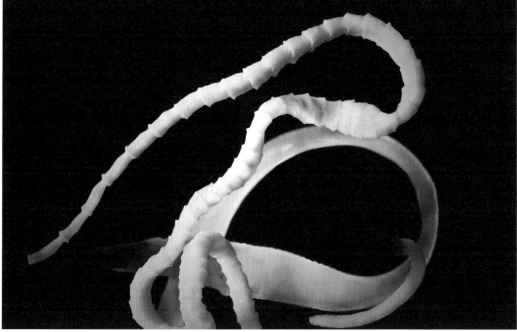

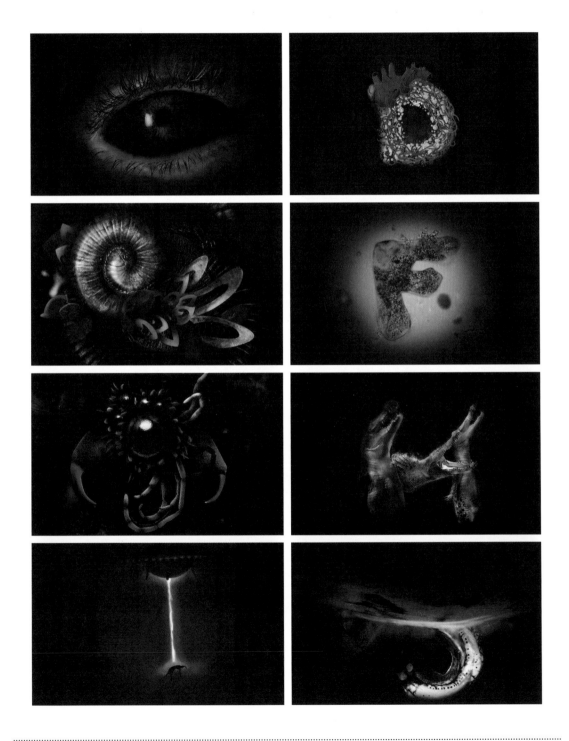

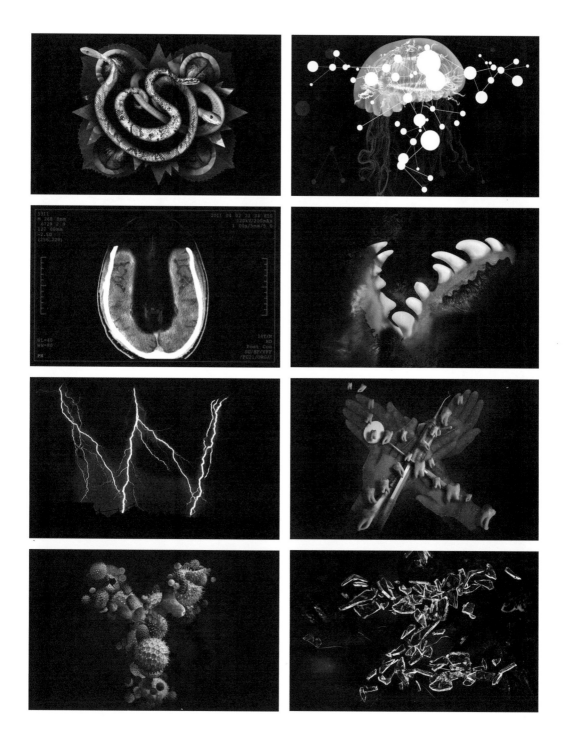

Micro Type

Ruslan Khasanov

After Ruslan Khasanov made his first liquid type, he had obtained a lot of different textures which looked beautifully like clusters of microorganisms under a microscope with their fantastic shapes and bright colours. *Micro Type* is a derivation of the idea, with mixed ink and explored forms.

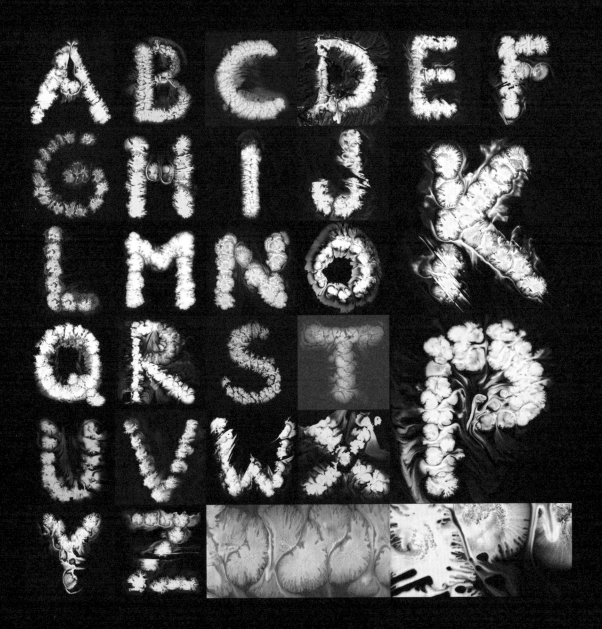

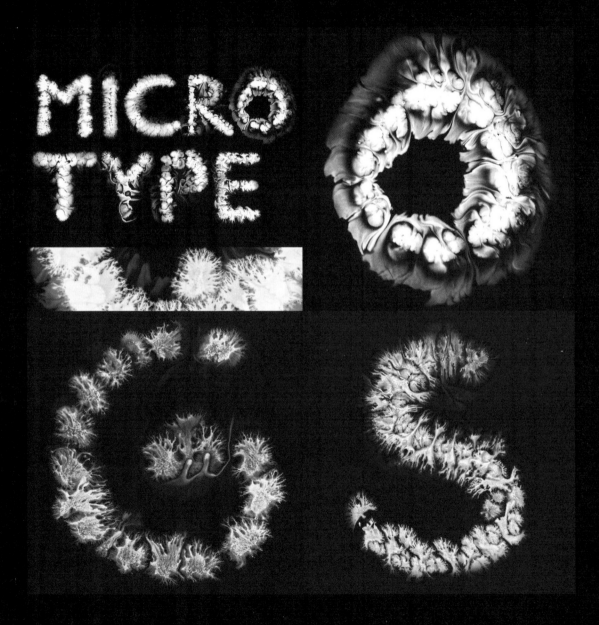

Au Revoir

Ruslan Khasanov

Having begun with the writing of the letter 'D' with a wet brush on a wet sink for a wine, *Au Revoir* are dynamic ink letters that are flowing in patterns before disappearing, like the short life cycle of butterflies. The final versions are realised on wet paper captured by camera.

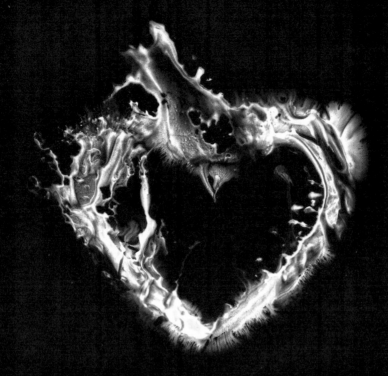

AU REVOIR

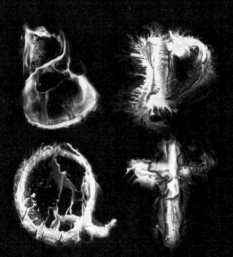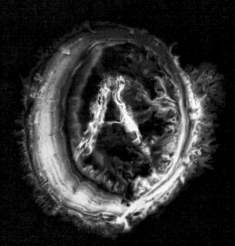

BIOGRAPHY

A is a name

F•016-017, 046-047, 150-153, 164-167

A is a name consists of Simon Renaud and Jérémie Nuel is a studio based in Paris, France. They put the notion of evolution in their design process as a cycle of graphic research concentrated on typographic systems.

Akatre

F•040-045

Founded by Valentin Abad, Julien Dhivert and Sebastien Riveron, Akatre is a graphic design studio based in Paris, France which works in visual identities, edition, photography, spaces on all medias.

Akatre works mainly for cultural and luxury projects for CNAP, Galerie des Galeries (Lafayette' galleries), the theater TU Nantes, Issey Miyake, Kenzo, etc. Akatre collaborates with galeries, choreographers and artists like Cindy Van Acker, Perrine Valli, Seulgi Lee, and creates for all its projects typographies and visuals (photo). They believe it is an essential process to create and offer a personal point of view about a project.

Akpem, Senongo

A•066-069

A Nigerian-American web designer and art director based in New York, Akpem does everything from interaction design to experimental typeface design, with a little printmaking mixed in. He probably thinks about sci-fi the rest of the time.

Alessandra, Amandine

A•010-011, 030-031, 054-055

Amandine Alessandra is a freelance photographer and graphic designer based in London, UK. After a Master in Fine Arts & Aesthetics from the Université de Provence in France, she moved to the UK where she graduated with a Master in Graphic Design from the London College of Communication in 2009.

Since setting up her practice in January 2010, she's been freelancing with agencies based in Paris, Lisbon, New York and Los Angeles. A contributor to numerous publications, she is also a visiting lecturer at Bedfordshire University and London College of Communication.

Alves, Sérgio

F•154-157

An emerging young designer based in the city of Porto, northern Portugal. Sérgio's designs are not limited to a specific school or idea, but rather often based on arts and crafts or use of organic materials within the design process. Each project may differ greatly from the next as he experiments with new mediums and allows each project to dictate the best way to communicate.

His main focuses have been on creating posters for cultural events, which allow for greater experimentation and creativity. He also has some projects with editorial design and corporate identity.

Autobahn

F•202-203

Autobahn is Jeroen Breen (1981), Maarten Dullemeijer (1982) and Rob Stolte (1981) who graduated from Utrecht School of the Arts (HKU). Autobahn designs special graphical projects, often with an illustrative and typographical angle. Autobahn is characterised by an analytical approach in the beginning and a strong sense of form at the end of the process, combined with passion and ambition.

Banton, Brian

A•018-019

Brian Banton is a freelance graphic designer and part-time faculty member of the Department of Design at York University. He holds a Master of Design from York University and Bachelor of Design from the Ontario College of Art and Design (now OCADU) in Toronto, Canada.

His work has been recognised by The Art Directors Club of New York, The Advertising and Design Club of Canada and The Adobe Design Achievement Awards.

Beato, André

F•058-059

André Beato is Portuguese graphic designer and Illustrator, born in Lisbon and currently based in London working as a freelancer.

With a BA Graphic Design and a Master in Design Visual Culture - Visual Production at IADE (Instituto de Artes Visuais e Marketing) in Lisbon, his work is mostly vector based graphics, corporate identities and illustrated typography.

He has been working in various creative fields of graphic, print and editorial, collaborating with clients from various industries such as record labels, magazines, clothing companies, advertising and others.

His work can be seeing in many publications and all over the web with a client list that ranges from Nike, MTV, Carhartt, ESPN, Montana Cans among others.

Bravo Company

A•034-035

Bravo Company is a creatively led, independent design studio based in Singapore. Working with a variety of individuals and organisations to deliver considered and engaging design, the team specialises in identity & brand development and printed communications & art direction.

Bureau Bruneau (Ludvig Bruneau Rossow)

A•016-017, F•084-085

Bureau Bruneau is the one man show of Ludvig Bruneau Rossow, a 24-year-old designer from Oslo, Norway. He mainly works with printed matter ranging from visual identities to editorial design and packaging. The ideas behind his projects varies from technical to emotional concepts. Rossow graduated from the Graphic Design department at Westerdals School of Communication in 2010. After working at Uniform for one year, he did an internship at Sagmeister Inc. in New York. Rossow is currently working at Bleed in Oslo, Norway.

Capener, Andrew

F•010-011

Andrew Capener is the cofounder of 755 Marketing and of kneadbe.com: "Your Allergen & Gluten Free Marketplace". He is a lover of the arts and an internet entrepreneur.

Chang, Bianca

F•012-015

Bianca Chang is a young designer, artist and image maker based in Sydney, Australia. After studying at the Queensland College of Art, she started her career working as an editorial designer in Singapore before relocating to Sydney. Armed with a love of type and wanting to explore it in three dimensions, she started working on a series of hand-cut graphic paper sculptures which she has since exhibited and continues to develop through gallery shows and private commissions.

Chris Nixon Design

F•048-049

Chris Nixon is a young and enthusiastic designer who loves exploring and developing new means for self-expression through the medium of typography and design. His style has developed to create an array of striking typographical quotes and phrases heavily focused around the use of juxtaposition to create a fresh and imaginative portfolio.

Corgier, Jerome

A•026-027, F•052-053

Jerome Corgier is a French freelance graphic designer and the founder of Atelier Pariri. He is particularly interested in sculptural typographic works and illustrations with that Books Covers, brands. Corgier began his career in Los Angeles by April Greiman, when he opened his eyes to the use of type as a creative item and not only as a concept. Corgier's goal is to give life inside letters.

Dan Tobin Smith Studio

F•192-197

Represented by Art Partner, British photographer Dan Tobin Smith, who received education at Central St. Martin, UK and London College of Printing, UK, gains inspirations from Seiju Toda, Lennart Nilsson, Josef Sudek amongst others.

He has been commissioned for Acne Paper, Another, China Vogue, Creative Review, Grafik, i-D, New York Times Magazine, Numero Homme, Wallpaper*, etc. and serving a contrasting client base including Absolut, Bacardi, British Airways, Coca-Cola, Honda, Nike, Orange, Shell, Sony, Volkswagen, etc. He is now based in the gritty eastern tip of London.

www.dantobinsmith.com
www.alphabetical.org

Delort, Pierre

F•176-177

Pierre Delort was born in Avignon, France in 1082. He studied graphic design in Marseille. After receiving his diploma, Delort started his own studio as an independent graphic designer. In 2009 he was honoured as the laureate of the French section of the 14th Biennial of young artists from Europe and the Mediterranean.

Delort worked on the French communication of the Biennial for two years which gave him the opportunity to be free with his creations and to develop his own idea of graphic design and typography. To him, letters and words are an enormous, quasi infinite playground!

Egan, Joseph & Thomson, Hunter

F•198-201

Joseph Egan and Hunter Thomson are two design students who completed their Foundation Degree together at Chelsea College of Art & Design, London in June 2010. Since then Egan has progressed to the BA Honours courses in Graphic Design at Chelsea College of Art & Design whilst Thomson is now studying Law at the Nottingham University. Both designers continue to working towards their degrees, whilst simultaneously taking on new client-based work and collaborating with as many creative groups as possible.

Eggert, Alicia & Fleming, Mike

F•184-185

Alicia Eggert and Mike Fleming met in a drawing class at Drexel University in Philadelphia, where they earned their bachelor's degrees in Interior Design and Photography respectively. After college, Eggert pursued a career in architectural design, and Fleming became a freelance photographer and musician. They reconnected at a Friendsgiving dinner in 2008, while Eggert was back in school for an MFA in Sculpture at Alfred University. The fell in love and began collaborating in 2009, and have shown their work in Milan, Philadelphia, New York City, Portland (ME), and Alfred (NY). They currently reside in Bruncwick, Maine. They are still in love.

e-Types

F•028-033

e-Types is a strategic brand and design agency that moves companies and organisations forward through identity. Brand leadership is characterised by the clear signals of an organisation permeated by a strong sense of identity and purpose. e-Types illuminates corporate ideas. Through brand strategy and graphic design embedded in big ideas, they nurture enthusiasm, increase sales and enhance leadership.

Family

F•158-159

Family is an award winning graphic design studio, providing a unique and different approach to sectors such as music, fashion, culture and the arts. The team is also interested in collaborating with other designers and creative's in various sectors.

Form Follows Freedom

A•028-029

Sara Ivanyi is an autonomous designer. Her multidisciplinary studio Form Follows Freedom was founded in Amsterdam in 2009. She works with a network of talented professionals to realise commissioned as well as self-initiated projects including lighting and product design, site specific installation, works for the public space and creative concepts for museums and theatres.

Fascinated by grids and natural phenomenon, she investigates where the two and three dimensional come to define each other. Examining where concept becomes experience, her designs are completed by their interaction with their user or surroundings.

Happycentro

F•066-077

The studio began in 1998 in Verona, the romantic city of Romeo and Juliet. In recent years, Happycentro has worked with both large and small clients, for local agencies and major international companies. Their approach to design is always the same: designing a logo, an advertising page, a wall or directing a commercial offering the same opportunity to deal with a problem. With time the studio has become quite good at solving problems.

Mixing complexity, order and fatigue is Happycentro's formula for beauty. Always, in addition to the commissioned work, the team spends plenty of energy in research and testing. Visual art, typography, graphic design, illustration, animation, film direction and music, the team likes contamination between creative disciplines and diversity in general. They don't like to do the same thing twice and prefer to go beyond what they are already able to do. It is tiring but satisfied. Happycentro are: Roberto Solieri, Federico Galvani, Giulio Grigollo, Andrea Manzati and the photographer Federico Padovani.

HelloMe

A•032-033, F•022-023, 086-089, 148-149

HelloMe is a Berlin-based design studio focusing on art direction, graphic design and typography.

With a systematic design approach the studio creates and implements innovative communication strategies and distinctive dynamic visual systems for cultural, social and business clients. The studio's mentality is ideas led, project specific and grounded on analytic thinking.

HelloMe believes design is experimental, dynamic and useful. They approach each commission from a cross-media perspective, and emphasise the intrinsic characteristics of each project to create innovative, well-crafted design solutions and self-initiated projects with a passion for detail and typography.

Hutchens, Jenny Kyvik

A•008-009

Jenny Kyvik Hutchens is a 23-year-old graphic design student, currently studying my third year at Westerdals School of Communication in Oslo, Norway.

Jethi, Nishant

A•024-025

After passing out from M. S. University, Baroda, in 2004, Nishant Jethi started his career as a visualiser at Everest Brand Solutions. He had won a Silver Pencil Oneshow, a Cannes Bronze and the London International (2005-06) for an outdoor installation for Cancer Patients Aid Association.

After three years at Everest, Jethi moved to Leo Burnett as an art director. He was nominated at D&AD Inbook and won a Cannes Silver in Design and Cannes Bronze in Promo out of the total 12 nominations he received. He also received four nominations in One Show in 2010.

In 2010, Jethi moved to Mudra communication pvt .Ltd. Mumbai, India and started working on

Living Typography, which was nominated for the Cannes Festival (2010). *Living Typography* was a promotional project for Water Design Studio.

Jiggery Pokery

F•171

Anna Lomax and Lauren Davies AKA Jiggery Pokery apply playful imagination, unbeatable hunter-gatherer skills and excellent scalpel and gaffa tape precision to bring their ideas to life. Fascinated by inventions, the bizarre, pop-culture, psychedelia, pound shops, glitter and shine, Lomax and Davies are constantly seeking the next challenge. Putting their stamp on a wide spectrum of disciplines ranging from window displays to music videos, editorial shoots to promotional campaigns, studio exhibitions to interior design along with ongoing self-initiated projects, they aim to leave no creative terrain unmarked. They have worked on projects for clients such as Beck's, Topshop, Creative Review, The Independent, Nike, SHOWstudio, Vauxhall and YCN.

Kawamura, Masashi

F•106-109

Masashi Kawamura was born in Tokyo and raised in San Francisco. He is the founder and creative director of the Creative Lab, PARTY, in Tokyo and New York. Previously he was the creative director at Wieden+Kennedy New York, and has worked in various international agencies such as BBH London and 180 Amsterdam.

Kawamura has produced numerous award winning global ad campaigns for brands such as adidas, Levi's, Nokia, Unilever, Sony, Google, and more. Outside of advertising, he has been exploring on the possibilities of design and interaction on personal projects including music videos, books, games, and TV shows. He was recently chosen as the Creativity magazine's 2011 Creative 50.

Khasanov, Ruslan

A•070-073, F134-135

Ruslan Khasanov is a freelance designer and an art director from Yekaterinburg, Russia. He graduated from Ural State Academy of Architecture and Arts and got a bachelor degree. Except graphic design and art, he also loves cinema as his old passion and hopes to make a movie one day. Currently he works on the experimental projects and runs his own studio.

KOTENHITS

A•012-015

Takashi Kawada is the CEO and art director of product design studio KOTENHITS which he founded in 2005. Kawada does art direction for various creations ranging from graphic, web,

visual and products. In 2007, he jointly started the creative group HITSFAMILY and launched "HITSPAPER" with Arata Sasaki of HITSME. The duo is at the forefront of today's creative scene. In 2008, Kawada took on as art director and graphic designer for Daisy Balloon.

Ku, Eric

F•054-055

Eric Ku, a graphic designer / artist who currently lives and works in NYC.

Landry, Jean-Maxime

F•008

He is a graphic design student at the University of Quebec in Montreal, Canada.

LoSiento

F•004-005

After starting his career in Industrial Design at Escola de Disseny Elisava, Barcelona, Borja Martínez moved to London in 1999 to study Graphic Design at the London College of Printing (today, London College of Communication).

He returned to Barcelona and, in 2005, founded LoSiento, where he started developing different graphic design and art direction projects. Nowadays, LoSiento gathers a team of 5 professionals and continues to work in design projects from the fields of corporative, packaging, editorial and carrying out personal projects as well.

The studio is especially interested in taking over identity projects as a whole. LoSiento's work is a physical approach to the graphic solutions, resulting in a field where graphic and industrial design go hand by hand, always searching for alliances with the artisans process.

Mark Gowing Design

F•168-169

Mark Gowing has been a design professional since 1987. His work has been awarded, exhibited and published around the world. In 2008 Gowing became the first Australian to win the Gold Medal at the 21st International Poster Biennale in Warsaw, which led to a feature exhibition at the Biennale in 2010. Gowing is the director of Mark Gowing Design and curator of the AGDA Poster Annual.

me studio

F•050-051, 098-099

me studio is a (very) small, independent graphic design studio founded in 2005 in Amsterdam and run by Martin Pyper, a British designer who studied in France and at art school in the UK,

speaks fluent French and Dutch, and has lived in The Netherlands since 1989.

me studio's work always comprises a mix of three things: image, identity and inspiration. This usually results in corporate identities, posters and books for a range of cultural and commercial clients in all kinds of sectors such as the dutch national ballet, theater companies, publishing companies, film production companies and non-profit clients. Their client list include big and small companies like Foot Locker, Vodafone, BMW, Ford, Postbank, ABN AMRO bank, The City of Amsterdam, Heineken, MTV, Nike, British Airways, Shell, EMI and charities like 'doctors without borders' & 'dance 4 life', individuals, artists, photographers and even the occasional odd job for free for members of our families and friends.

me studio has won numerous awards and nominations, their work has been published in various books and magazines. Their projects have been added to the permanent collection of the 'Stedelijk Museum' for modern art in Amsterdam. Martin Pyper was one of the co-founders of the 'mind the gap' design seminar series in Amsterdam, he has been a board member of the dutch art directors association (ADCN), the Dutch photographers association (PANL) and has had work displayed in several large international exhibitions including 'the favourites' — by 25 dutch designers in Bucharest, Romania in 2006, the chicago international poster biennial 2010 and 'messages to the world' an international poster exhibition in Shanghai 2010.

Mentxaka, Txaber

A•042-049

Txaber was born in Bilbao, Spain. After studying graphic design, 1988-1992, has developed an intense professional life as a graphic designer working for different agencies and a large range of clients. Experimentation is a constant note in its evolution as a designer, resulting in remarkable work and high technical quality.

Morel, Julie

F•078-079

Julie Morel is an artist born in Lyon, France. Her work explores and questions the everyday relations between humans and technologies. Her art projects are often text based and challenge the viewers by turning them into readers.

She has exhibited her work in national and international venues. She is part of the net.art collective incident.net since 1998 and is the creator/curator of the art in residence program "Géographies variables". She teaches contemporary art and new media practice, as well as being the Head of Research of the "Auto-immediate archiving" research program at the EESAB (European Fine art school in Brittany, France).

NAM

A•056-059, F•170

NAM is a Tokyo-based graphic/art collective, formed in May 2006 by a graphic designer Takayuki Nakazawa and a photographer Hiroshi Manaka. Currently a team of more than 10 artists, NAM creates works with hints of fantasy, fusing graphic design point of view into photographic expression.

National Forest Design

F•110-115

A design firm and creative consultancy seeing themselves as both innovative thinkers and visual engineers. Their approach to communication is holistic and spans a wide spectrum of disciplines from art direction, photography, advertising and graphic design to illustration, web design, film, and art.

At the core, the people of National Forest are dedicated to making the world a better place. They feel compelled to share the fun, beauty, and excitement they have been fortunate enough to experience in hopes of encouraging others to enjoy life, foster love and empathy, and make stronger, more sincere connections.

Nicolausson, Martin

F•056-057

Martin Nicolausson is perhaps the only Swedish illustrator and graphic designer with the name Martin Nicolausson. This is important as originality is one of his most admired principles. As a child he would spend equal amounts of time questioning adults and drawing on his guinea pigs face. These dramatic tensions can be seen in his present work. This work has been described as naturally and artificially flavoured and he wouldn't have it any other way. Recognised as an ADC Young Guns winner in 2010, he counts Absolut Vodka, The Economist, Topman and The New York Times amongst his clients.

Pastor, Joan Ramon

A•050-053

Joan Ramon Pastor, also known as Wete, is a Spanish graphic designer based in Barcelona. Painting graffiti since his childhood, Pastor loves letterforms, typography and believes in the complexity of easy things. He also works at the Spanish studio Vasava.

Plasticbionic

F•116-118, 124-127, 132-133

Animated by his love for the type, the creative director and graphic designer, Plasticbionic lives in Nantes, France. He works as a freelancer and works for studios or agencies like Serial Cut™ in Madrid, McCann San Francisco, Amuse-

ment Magazine, Computer Art, etc. In perpetual graphic research, he loves creating and experimenting with typography and illustration. With an evident taste for simple geometric shapes, his areas of expertise include art direction, illustration, graphic design, web design, concept development, typography, and 3D design.

Plenty

A•040-041, F•090-091

Plenty, from Buenos Aires (ARG), is the brainchild of Pablo Alfieri and Mariano Farias. Thanks to this merger and the help and involvement of a slew of other talented professionals Plenty has become one of the leading motion graphics agencies.

Plenty's work has been featured in magazines and blogs such as Stash, Computer Love and Motionographer and their client list includes the likes of Fox International, MTV Latin America and International, VH1, Nat Geo, Chandon, Schweppes Australia, Doritos Brazil and Vodafone and those are just some recent additions.

Plenty's vast experience, flexibility in assembling multidisciplinary teams and inexhaustible passion are the qualities that define Plenty and ensure their success and that of their customers.

Plenty's work is mesmerising and colourful with a touch of futuristic landscapes, shapes and textures. Almost like an explosion of design, each piece shows off their multifaceted nature and talented teamwork.

Rioux, Pier-Phillipe

F•009

Pier-Phillipe Rioux is a graphic design student at the University of Quebec in Montreal, Canada.

Roots

F•100-101

An interdisciplinary graphic design studio based in Singapore, Roots produces captivating, intelligent and beautifully crafted design with forward thinking ideas and executions.

Ruhry, Valentin

F•190-191

Artist Valentin Ruhry was born in Graz, Austria in 1982. He is a technically well versed do-it-yourselfer with a profound wit, a distinctive propensity to experiment and a penchant for subtle deeper meaning. The objects he creates have a lot to do with the everyday world surrounding us. He engages in it and changes it to allow a new perspective on the world of things.

He is a new style object artist, who handles his materials with passion, creates new items in a playful way, thus making clear formal as well as content related statements.

Ruhry is rooted in an art historic tradition where he is successful at creating independent workers of art. Some of his creations give a sense of reverberation of the era of ready-mades, the Arte Povera and the conceptual and media art.

Sabatini, Riccardo

A•036-039

Riccardo Sabatini was born the March 1983, in Pescia, Italy. He's a graphic designer and digital artist currently based in Florence, Italy.

He has always been interested in all kinds of arts since the early childhood, then developing through the years an eclectic style between graphic design and digital art, especially in his personal projects.

After graduated in graphic design at the international design academy Accademia Italiana in Florence, he has started to work as freelance for several clients, in his own city and internationally, through the web, and at the same time carrying on a lot of personal projects such as Mekkanika, the typeface featured in this book.

Sawdust

F•160-163

Sawdust is the award-winning creative partnership of Rob Gonzalez and Jonathan Quainton. They are an independent graphic design duo based in London. Their disciplines include art direction, image-making and typography across music, art, culture, fashion corporate and advertising sectors.

Sawdust's approach has earned them a worldwide reputation for creating visually striking work that is thoughtful, innovative and meticulously crafted. Their work has been featured in internationally recognised publications including D&AD, Novum Lürzer's Archive, IdN, Gallery, Computer Arts, Print and Los Logos: Compass.

Sayer, Alida Rosie

F•178-183

Alida Rosie Sayer is a London-based visual designer and artist working across the fields of typography, 3D-design, animation and illustration. Recent projects have ranged from fashion and music branding to highly experimental self-initiated sculptural works and exhibitions.

A prominent feature of Sayer's work is the layering of information in order to reveal simultaneous depths that might not normally be visible. She is particularly interested in seeking to express visually what cannot be communicated using either words or pictures alone, often treating letterforms as tactile objects and manipulating them in order to alter or enhance their meaning.

Scheiger, Andreas

F•092-097

Born 1963 in Vienna, Scheiger studied economics and business administration. A part time illustrator for various magazines, Scheiger finished studies in 1990 and started work in biggest Austrian advertising agency where he was later promoted as an art director. It was the advertising time out for Scheiger in 2002 and he acquired diving vessel in Egypt where he lived until 2008. He reentered creative advertising in 2008 and has been working on private creative graphic design projects besides work.

Schwen, David

F•034-037

David Schwen is currently working as an art director and designer in Minneapolis, USA. Previous studio experience has included Mono, Fallon, and Carmichael Lynch. David works in a wide range of styles and is experienced in illustration, design, interactive, apparel and motion graphics. His list of clients includes Apple, Nike, Disney, Fox, Harley-Davidson, Nestle, Target and Threadless.

Serial Cut™

F•119-123, 128-129

Serial Cut™ is a Madrid based studio, established in 1999 by Sergio del Puerto, working on a wide variety of worldwide projects, but focusing mainly on art direction for big and small companies from arts and culture, fashion or entertainment industries. For each new project from a given client, the team likes to change the look and feel of the design.

Shimizu, Ryo

F•186-189

Ryo Shimizu is drawn to the relation between social classes and cultural capital. He creates works which use letters and symbols to reconstruct classifications that people make partly unconsciously in everyday life, for instance, a dichotomy into the friendly and the hostile, and ambiguous and bipolar relationships oscillating between the terms of such binary classifications.

Skyrill.com

A•020-021

Skyrill.com is a fusion of two brothers, Hussain and Ali Almossawi, from Bahrain. The duo started their company in 2009, and has been working since on great projects and with great clients. Alongside commercial work, they also work on personal projects and experimentations, such as the Type Fluid Experiment. They believe that type is an essential part of design, and can play an important role in shaping the final outcome.

Soon

F•172-175

Soon is a Belgian studio that creates visual identities in combination with photography. Most of their work is hand crafted and afterwards transformed into a digital image. It's some arts and crafts combined with modern techniques.

Soon builds total identities including corporate, event, editorial, etc. in a creative way, combining handcraft with good photography. Soon wants things to be perfect. Their customer base spans cultural, industrial, medical, governmental and other sectors.

Soon does not really have one dream project. Every project that allows them to create something in a decent amount of time, freedom of creativity and with sufficient funds is a dream project for them. At the end of the road it is important that the customer shakes their hand and tells them he is satisfied or blown by the end result.

Studiowill

F•102-105

Founded in 2009 by Joe Kwan, Studiowill is a Hong Kong-based design studio specialising in print, branding, corporate identity, packaging, environmental graphic, etc. With a great passion for what they do, Studiowill is fresh and motivated. The studio always base their projects on knowledge about client's reality. Simple, clean, and flesh, Studiowill creates crafted graphic design for open-minded people.

Superexpresso

F•064-065

Superexpresso is Italian-born Michele Angelo who studied painting, visual and industrial design and later moved to work as a graphic designer in Barcelona. He is currently working as a freelance designer, still spending his life on his weird creatures full of love at night.

Angelo believes in a hand-crafted approach to design and loves the contrast between modern tools and classic "human" techniques. He likes to experiment with new ways more than following existing trends and believes the approach can be used in all fields and offer interesting new solutions depending on the project.

Taku Satoh Design Office Inc.

F•006-007

Taku Satoh is the graphic designer behind. His creative activities are varied, spanning product design, commercial design, branding, planning of exhibition, art direction and general direction of TV program on educational channel.

There Is

F•136-143

A love for words and beautiful images led Sean Freeman to explore a harmony of both, spreading his wings to up his own studio: There Is, specialising in creative typography, illustration and art direction.

Based in East London, Freeman creates award winning typographic treatments and illustrations for a varied range of clients globally from advertising to music, editorial and publishing; with his work being featured in numerous books and magazines around the world. His work is known to be as powerful as it is unique: a dynamic and organic fusion between elements.

Forever curious, Freeman is constantly exploring new ways of approaching his work with a love for happy accidents and a passion for visual storytelling, texture, type and everything in between.

Toby And Pete

F•130-131

Toby and Pete is a creative craft shop that consists of a select team of directors, creatives and designers. They collaborate on all briefs to create conceptually rich and visually innovative work.

Toledo, Mico

F•024-027

Mico Toledo is an art director with 9 years experience in advertising. He studied at Central Saint Martins School of Design and he is currently working at Mother London as a creative where he is responsible for creating campaigns for Stella Artois, Boots and Becks. Music Philosophy is his side project where he gets philosophical part of songs and turns them into beautifully designed posters.

Torafu Architects

F•204-207

Founded in 2004 by Koichi Suzuno and Shinya Kamuro, Torafu Architects employs a working approach based on architectural thinking. Works by the duo include a diverse range of products, from architectural design to interior design for shops, exhibition space design, product design, spatial installations and film making.

Torafu Architects has received many prizes including the Design for Asia (DFA) Grand Award for the "TEMPLATE IN CLASKA" in 2005, and the Grand Prize of the Elita Design Awards 2011 with "Light Loom (Milano Salone 2011)".

The airvase book and TORAFU ARCHITECTS Ideas + Process 2004-2011 were published in 2011.

Tsto Creative

F•018-021

Tsto is a creative consultancy founded by Johannes Ekholm, Jonatan Eriksson, Inka Järvinen, Matti Kunttu, Jaakko Pietiläinen and Antti Uotila, a team of graphic design professionals specialised in coming up with ideas and visualising them. Their approach is thorough and hands-on. They tackle an assignment by first taking it apart to its bare essentials, and then building it in a new way that best serves the client. This design philosophy let's them go deeper than the surface, to the essence of each case. Tsto also works with other proven professionals in whatever media the work requires.

Vallée, Julien

F•146-147

Julien Vallée is a Montreal based artist and designer working in a wide range of fields, such as art direction, motion graphics, print design, art installation as well as film and design for the television industry. Trying to explore the different fields of design, he's been questioning the relative roles of the computer and handmade processes in design. He tries to get in touch with every aspect of the environment, using manual processes strongly supported by the technological tools of today to bridge as many of these disciplines as he can. Through his plastic experimentations and projects for his clients such as the New York Times, AOL, Swatch and MTV, he tends to reinvest image synthesis technologies, mainly in mixing digital conception phase with fragile implementation material, such as paper and cardboard.

Walsh, Jessica

F•080-083

Jessica Walsh is a multidisciplinary designer living and working in NYC. She has been named Computer Arts magazines "Top Rising Star in Design," an Art Directors Club "Young Gun" and Print Magazines "New Visual Artist." She has worked with studios such as Sagmeister Inc, Pentagram Design and Print magazine and freelances for a variety of clients such as The New York Times, AIGA, Computer Arts, I.D. Magazine, Technology Review, and many others. When not doing design she can be found playing with her dog momo, eating avocados, or doing yoga.

Whitton, Stuart

A•006-007

Stuart Whitton began to express himself creatively at a young age, by drawing various elements from his imagination and his surroundings. Using traditional mediums he creates imagery tailored to his perceptions. A careful discretion of detail is utilised to develop a visually appealing relationship between meticulously drawn ethereal illustrations of the human form, objects and typographical elements.

His influences lie in the process of image construction, form, and surreal ambiguity with a preference towards detailed tonal qualities true to the realistic. The work is a direct representation of his personality and inspiration, which can be identified in the smallest details.

Yonenaga, Itaru / NO CONTROL AIR

F•106-109

Fashion designer born in Kyoto, Japan, 1979.

Youda, Yoriko

A•060-065

By visualising Japanese and Chinese Asian culture, Youda contemplates the meaning of traditional art in modern times. Her theme is "Adeyaka", it means fascinating and elegant in Japanese.

Her art work includes both digital and analogue materials. Youda has been participated in various domestic and international exhibitions. She is currently based in Japan.

YouWorkForThem

F•144-145

YouWorkForThem is one of the best design brands in the world. Their clients include Apple, Wieden + Kennedy, EMI, Victoria's Secret, Nike, Diesel, Burton Snowboards, ABC News, Gap, BMW, Epitaph Records, Starbuck's Coffee, Wired Magazine, Cartoon Network, Sony Music, Coca-Cola, Puma, Samsung, Harvard University, Element Skateboards, American Airlines, Warner Brothers and the band U2.

Zaech, Juri

F•060-063

Juri Zaech is a typographer and art director working and living in Paris. After his studies in typography he worked in Switzerland for a couple of years before he went to an international advertising school in Hamburg.

Zim&Zou

A•022-023, F•038-039

Zim&Zou is a French graphic design studio based in Nancy, France. Composed of Lucie Thomas and Thibault Zimmermann who studied graphic design in an art school. The studio proposes a contemporary approach of design. Thanks to a mix of different fields such as paper sculpture, installation, graphic design, and illustration, Zim&Zou's strength is to be a complementary and polyvalent duo.

First published and distributed by
viction:workshop ltd.

viction:ary™

viction:workshop ltd.
Unit C, 7/F, Seabright Plaza, 9-23 Shell Street,
North Point, Hong Kong
Url: www.victionary.com   Email: we@victionary.com
www.facebook.com/victionworkshop
www.weibo.com/victionary

Edited and produced by viction:workshop ltd.

Concepts & art direction by Victor Cheung
Book design by viction:workshop ltd.
Cover artwork by Yoriko Youda and Martin Nicolausson

©2012 viction:workshop ltd.
Copyright on text and design work is held by respective
designers and contributors.

All rights reserved. No part of this publication may be
reproduced, stored in retrieval systems or transmitted in any
form or by any means, electronic, mechanical, photocopying,
recording or any information storage, without written
permissions from respective copyright owner(s).

All artwork and textual information in this book are based on the
materials offered by designers whose work has been included.
While every effort has been made to ensure their accuracy,
viction:workshop does not accept any responsibility, under any
circumstances, for any errors or omissions.

ISBN 978-988-19439-9-6

Printed and bound in China

Acknowledgements

We would like to thank all the designers and companies who have involved in the
production of this book. This project would not have been accomplished without
their significant contribution to the compilation of this book. We would also like to
express our gratitude to all the producers for their invaluable opinions and assis-
tance throughout this entire project. The successful completion also owes a great
deal to many professionals in the creative industry who have given us precious
insights and comments. And to the many others whose names are not credited but
have made specific input in this book, we thank you for your continuous support
the whole time.

Future Editions

If you wish to participate in viction:ary's future projects and publications, please
send your website or portfolio to submit@victionary.com